T0338196

MIGRANT LABOR IN CHINA ——

China Today series

MIGRANT LABOR IN CHINA

Post-Socialist Transformations

Pun Ngai

polity

First published in 2016 by Polity Press

Polity Press
65 Bridge Street
Cambridge CB2 1UR, UK

Polity Press
350 Main Street
Malden, MA 02148, USA

ISBN-13: 978-0-7456-7174-1
ISBN-13: 978-0-7456-7175-8(pb)

A catalogue record for this book is available from the British Library.

Library of Congress Cataloging-in-Publication Data

Pun, Ngai, 1970-
    Migrant labor in China : post-socialist transformation / Pun Ngai.
       pages   cm
    Includes bibliographical references and index.
    ISBN 978-0-7456-7174-1 (hardback) – ISBN 978-0-7456-7175-8 (pbk.)
1. Migrant labor–China.   2. Labor market–China.   3. Manpower policy–China.
4. Rural-urban migration–China.   5. China–Economic conditions–2000-
6. China–Economic policy–2000-   I. Title.
    HD5856.C5P864 2016
    331.5′440951–dc23
                                                                    2015032717

Typeset in 11.5 on 15 pt Adobe Jenson Pro
by Toppan Best-set Premedia Limited
Printed and bound in Great Britain by Clay ltd, St Ives PLC

For further information on Polity, visit our website:
politybooks.com

Contents

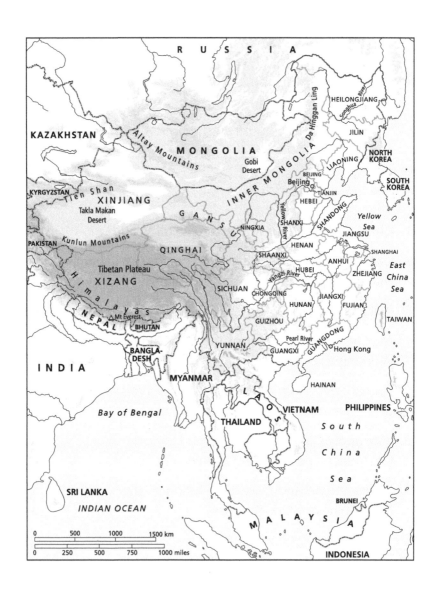

Chronology

March 1959	Tibetan Uprising in Lhasa; Dalai Lama flees to India
1959–61	Three Hard Years, widespread famine with tens of millions of deaths
1960	Sino–Soviet split
1962	Sino–Indian War
October 1964	First PRC atomic bomb detonation
1966–76	Great Proletarian Cultural Revolution; Mao reasserts power
February 1972	President Richard Nixon visits China; "Shanghai Communiqué" pledges to normalize US–China relations
September 1976	Death of Mao Zedong
October 1976	Ultra-Leftist Gang of Four arrested and sentenced
December 1978	Deng Xiaoping assumes power; launches Four Modernizations and economic reforms
1978	One-child family planning policy introduced
1979	US and China establish formal diplomatic ties; Deng Xiaoping visits Washington
1979	PRC invades Vietnam
1982	Census reports PRC population at more than one billion
December 1984	Margaret Thatcher co-signs Sino–British Joint Declaration agreeing to return Hong Kong to China in 1997
1989	Tiananmen Square protests culminate in June 4 military crack-down
1992	Deng Xiaoping's Southern Inspection Tour re-energizes economic reforms
1993–2002	Jiang Zemin is president of PRC, continues economic growth agenda

November 2001	WTO accepts China as member
2002–12	Hu Jintao, General-Secretary CCP (and President of PRC from 2003)
2002–3	SARS outbreak concentrated in PRC and Hong Kong
2006	PRC supplants US as largest CO_2 emitter
August 2008	Summer Olympic Games in Beijing
2010	Shanghai World Exposition
2012	Xi Jinping appointed General-Secretary of the CCP (and President of PRC from 2013)

Acknowledgements

This book would not have been possible without the Chinese migrant workers who have been actively involved in many of the research projects. I am grateful for the trust and confidence of Chinese migrant workers who have shared their experiences, stories, and struggles not only with me, but also my colleagues and students. Many of the research projects were carried out with an enthusiastic team of colleagues and students. Lu Huilin, Guo Yuhua, and Shen Yuan are the most important collaborators who participated in the joint research projects over the past five years. Without their unfailing support, it would have been impossible to carry out most of the research projects.

I cannot imagine that I would have had enough courage to complete these years-long studies without the joys and tears shared with my students and colleagues, especially Zhang Huipeng, Li Dajun, Liang Zicun, Su Yihui, Fan Lulu, Li Changjiang, Tang Weifeng, Jin Shuheng, Deng Yunxue, Chen Hangying, Liu Ya, Wu Xiongwenqian, Anita Koo, Jack Qiu, Yan Hairong, Ben Ku, and many others.

In the course of research and writing, Chris Smith, Michael Burawoy, Peter Evans, Ralf Ruckus, Ferruccio Gambino, Devi Sacchetto, Rutvica Andrijasevic, Anita Chan, and Jonathan Unger have always provided critical thought, informed commentary, and warm encouragement. I am deeply grateful to their intellectual support and encouragement.

I am very grateful to SACOM (Students and Scholars Against Corporate Misbehavior), CWWN (The Chinese Working Women Network), and supporters including Debby Chan, Yiyi Cheng, Pui

Kwan Liang, Parry Leung, Sophia So, Vivien Yau, Ken Yau, Yun-chung Chen, Kenneth Ng, Choi Suet-wah, Lau Ka-mei, and Leung Shuk-mei. I am also thankful for the support of Emma Longstaff, Jonathan Skerrett, Elen Griffiths, and Ian Tuttle of Polity Press, who offered help throughout the production process of the whole manuscript.

Earlier versions of the chapters have been published in *Modern China*, *China Journal*, *Global Labour Journal*, *Work, Employment and Society*, and *Cultural Anthropology*, and I would like to thank the editors and reviewers of those journals. I also would like to acknowledge academic funding support from Hong Kong Polytechnic University, Hong Kong Polytechnic University-Peking University China Social Work Research Center, and Hong Kong Research Grant Council for the project, "A New Age of World Factory: Capital Expansion, the Role of State and Foxconn Production in China" (2012–2015).

Last but not least, I would like to thank deeply my family, especially my mother and my two brothers who never fail to provide me support in times of need.

1 | China and Its Labor in the Neoliberal World

Let's enter the workshop of the world with the guidance of Chinese migrant workers who are now the protagonists of the new working class. The new working class, comprising mainly internal rural migrant subjects, is of an entirely different nature to that of Maoist China, and these subjects are the sole concern of this book. I owe this writing to the new working class as she has continuously revealed her rich, reflexive, and sometimes contradictory lived experiences to me over the past two decades. The rich and vividly lived experiences of this class in terms of work organization, dormitory labor life, feeling of class and class action are key to understanding China in the neoliberal world. Unlike most postmodern literature, which criticizes Karl Marx's ideas about class, class is still the central concept of this book, providing an effective analytical weapon with which to discern the lives of the working class under the major contradictions of contemporary capitalism.

China has developed into the workshop of the world during the last three decades. It has reshaped the global economy of the twenty-first century and the world's history of labor. This great transformation is, however, a paradox of China's Revolution, which once strived to end the imperialism and capitalism that encroached on China's ancient soil (Blecher 2010; Perry and Selden 2010). To understand this paradox, we have to make sense of the lives of the Chinese laborers who are subjected to, as well as the subjects of, the workshop of the world. The rise of China as the "workshop of the world" in the age of globalization and the accompanying new working class comprising several hundred millions provides us with a non-western perspective to understand the importance of laboring subjects and their class in shaping the transformed space of global capitalism. As E. P. Thompson said, while we cannot calculate the emergence of the working class like the rising sun every day, we are compelled to this impossible project only because we now live in the neoliberal capitalism of the twenty-first century. This century called more to the "end of history" than to the creation of new laboring subjects that could challenge this history and potentially create a new one. The struggle to create this new laboring class by itself and for itself nevertheless is reshaping the future of class relations and their struggles not only in China, but throughout the world.

Thirty years of post-socialist transformation has completely transformed China, which has hooked up into the neoliberal world. A socialist nation that was once viewed as a developing country now shapes and poses a challenge to the global economy. Little attention has been paid, however, to the making of a new working class comprising more than 270 million peasant-workers, *nongmin gong* or *mingong*, and another 100 million laid-off state-enterprise workers who have now joined the new laboring subjects in all sorts of enterprises. At the start of the new millennium, China's "world factory" inevitably constitutes and is constituted by this new laboring class, which is structurally embedded with the control of capital and workers' resistance. To understand this new class and its resistance politics, we have to situate them in the development of global capitalism and its impact on China's socialist transformation as well as the dynamics of China's reform and opening up.

The golden age of western capitalism that had boomed since the Second World War ended with a series of economic crises from the 1970s onwards. The strategic reshaping of the global economy was the result of the acceleration of the "extended reproduction" of capitalism on a global scale in order to resolve the crisis of capital accumulation in the spheres of production and circulation, which has inevitably resulted in the contradictions of capitalism. Overproduction, increase of productivity, decline of interest rates, and technological innovation have created a shift of capital flows from manufacturing industries to property and financial sectors on the one hand, but also increasingly the concentration of capital in manufacturing sectors such as electronics and car industries on the other. Within the changing manufacturing sector, a delinking of branding, design, technological innovation, and factory production was observed. This delinking was magically reconnected by a global supply and production chain under the monopoly of transnational capital and world-renowned brands (Appelbaum 2008, 2011).

The extended reproduction of contemporary capitalism has contributed to a rapid remaking of class relations in China and the rest of the world. The advance of technology and information creates hypermobile flows of capital, and the transnationality of new labor continues to shatter existing class relations.

A fundamental error of western hegemony is the proclamation of the end of the "working class" and class conflicts (Clark and Lipset 1991, 2001; Gorz 1997; Houtman et al. 2009). This hegemony shapes western academia in almost all areas as well as through cultural colonization, and penetrates into the intellectual circles of the rest of the world. A farewell to "class" colludes with the "end of history" (Fukuyama 2006).

Yet a farewell to "class" by western academics and mainstream media did not make class relations obsolete in western societies, which are now confronting deep class conflicts characterized by great social inequalities, high rates of unemployment and life precariousness. Instead, the issues of class and class conflicts have been carried by global capital flight into Third World societies, putting China at the forefront of the struggle. The increase in real numbers of mass workers challenges the postmodern theories which claimed that the use of new technology and new modes of production had replaced the traditional class sub-jects (Hardt and Negri 2005). The U-turn to neoliberal capitalism has created an impact on the world, defeating the attempts of communist revolutions of the twentieth century and the golden age of the welfare capitalist system in the West. It has attempted to destroy the fruits of the socialist goals of promoting economic equality, human emancipa-tion, and people's democracy. This global creative destruction contin-ued until a neoliberal world finally arrived, and the reformed China is now part of it.

The triumph of a neoliberal world has signaled the opportunity for capital to invade the dreamland of socialist China in the form of large-scale investment and off-shore production. Starting at the end of the 1970s, global capital reached the stage of rapid expansion, destroying all potential barriers erected by non-capitalist or socialist nation-states for capital flows, technology transfer, expropriation of production materials and markets, and last but not the least, the use of abundant labor. The strategy of capital concentration or monopoly was achieved by penetrating into non-capitalist countries via a multiplication of the global supply and production chain. The best examples are provided by Apple and Foxconn, ranked 5th and 30th on the Global 500 list in 2014, respectively.

Today, if China is a dreamland for global capital looking for new forms of capital accumulation on an unimaginable pace and scale, we argue that a new working class comprising rural migrants and urban poor is being created, and they now form the new political subjects for potential resistance, shape the future of the labor movement in China, and provide a quest for world labor internationalism.

THE ADVENT OF THE WORKSHOP OF THE WORLD IN CHINA

In recent years the term 'workshop of the world' is commonly used to describe the capacity of China for global production. The concept of a workshop of the world can be understood only in the context of the extended reproduction of global capitalism to subsume the social life of non-capitalist nations. Global capitalism has won a victory in incorporating socialist regimes into its process of capital accumulation over the last century. With the opening of China and the arrival of global and private capital into the export processing zones in the early 1980s, socialist China was already being transformed into a market economy under the wave of industrial relocation from advanced capitalist countries to the global South. The Chinese state had also taken a lead in introducing pro-market initiatives and put huge effort into bringing the country into the World Trade Organization (WTO) and other world bodies. China is now well known as a "world factory," attracting transnational corporations (TNCs) to China from all over the world, especially from Hong Kong, Taiwan, Japan, Korea, the USA, and Western Europe.

Western governments, from the political left to the political right, admire China's economic achievement as evidenced by the iconic skylines in Beijing and Shanghai as well as the stunning financial figures reported by the media. From 2003, China has passed the US and become the world's largest foreign direct investment (FDI) destination country. In 2005 China became the world's third-largest trading country, surpassed only by the US and Germany. In 2006, China climbed to be the fourth-largest economy in the world in terms of GDP (US$2,226 billion), and in 2010 China surpassed Japan as the second-largest economy in the world. Alongside the dramatic economic growth in quantity, the manufacturing sector was also moving into high-end goods. Exports of electric, electronic, and high-tech products amounted to US$19,258 billion in 2013, which accounted for 87 percent of the total export value.[1] Today, China has become the world's top producer of more than 200 products, including garments, color TVs, washing machines, DVD players, cameras, refrigerators, air conditioners, motorcycles, microwave ovens, PC monitors, tractors, and bicycles.[2]

With 29 percent of the world's workforce, labor costs in this giant "global factory" are as low as one-sixth that of Mexico and one-fortieth that of the US (Lee 2002; Robinson 2010).[3] In 2013, China's GDP per capita (US$6,807) still ranked as low as 84th in the world.[4] This contradiction of rapid growth and cheap labor cost has attracted criticism of China's role in driving a 'race to the bottom' in globalization from labor researchers, labor activists, and journalists (Chan 2001, 2003; Friedman and Lee 2010; Scott 2012). China is one of the targets in Western campaigns against 'sweatshops'. Moreover, in recent years, media coverage on the rise and economic growth of China has aroused different feelings among Western workers and their organizations concerning the Chinese working class. 'Chinese workers steal our jobs' is one of the common myths for many. The US trade union federation, AFL-CIO, demanded that their government impose trade restrictions on China for being responsible for the disappearance of 2.5 million manufacturing jobs at home.[5] This is the backdrop to the "China Threat."

It has been widely recognized that workers around the world are pitted against each other in the game of "race to the bottom" production over who will accept the lowest wages and benefits, and the most miserable working and living conditions. In this game, China appears to have an impact on the wage level for the world's workers in labor-intensive export industrialization. While some Chinese specialists would argue that factory work as well as other forms of employment have largely improved the living standards of Chinese peasants, who otherwise would have to keep toiling in the rural countryside, this book looks into the actual situations of the new working class supported by solid field studies, detailed reports, and documentation. I have been involved in different research projects on migrant labor, especially ongoing studies on the lived experiences and struggles of workers in the construction, electronics, and textile and garment industries. Ethnographic data, including in-depth interviews, surveys, and semi-structured questionnaires are the most commonly used methods. Most of the field studies are conducted in multiple sites and are frequently revisited.

The rapid flight of global capital to China is nevertheless not only looking for cheap labor and low land prices, but also diligent, skilled, and well-educated Chinese internal migrant workers who are willing to work in appalling conditions, who are suitable for just-in-time production, and who are potential consumers for global products such as iPhones and iPads. The repositioning of China as a "workshop of the world" hence provides the bedrock for nurturing a new Chinese working class which is now spreading all over the country, on construction sites, in workplaces, and in companies and offices, irrespective of the nature of capital, sectors, and forms of work.

Global capital and the reformist state have jointly turned China into the "workshop of the world" over the past 30 years. This is the backdrop to the world workshop, and the new Chinese working class is now on the stage, living their working lives, and beginning their lifelong struggle. This book explores the emergence of the contemporary neoliberal form of global capitalism in China, which shapes the processes of industrialization and urbanization and structurally forms the new working class which has no choice but to go along with it or resist it in the long run.

THE U-TURN TO NEOLIBERALISM

One of the basic tenets of Marxism is that the capitalist system contains insurmountable contradictions. Both world wars were the result of the accumulated contradictions of the capitalist system in the twentieth century (Silver 2003). The wars allowed a temporary amelioration of these contradictions accumulated over the long term and led to a shift in the development strategy of the Anglo-American-led capitalist states, which made a series of adjustments to the capitalist system. In the post-war years US-extended Keynesianism has strengthened state intervention in the economy, with state investment funding a large number of government public works, increasing employment provision, offering subsidies to agriculture and raising the spending power of ordinary Americans. Furthermore, the social democracies of Europe, particularly the north European nations, instituted welfare state policies. Governments used redistributive policies, controls on the flow of capital and increased public spending to implement the so-called 'cradle to grave' welfare regimes. These welfare regimes succeeded to some extent in improving social welfare for the mass of the population, dampening down class conflict and helping maintain social order.

Yet whether it was Keynesian state intervention or welfare state policies, they have not challenged the interests of capital or the control of the monopoly capitalist class, partial adjustments of social redistribution made on the basis of leaving the mode of production and production relations untouched. Such adjustments could effect only a temporary amelioration of class antagonism and did not resolve the internal contradictions of capitalism – between socialized production and the private ownership of the means of production – at a fundamental level. This was why, by the 1970s, capitalism was finding it hard to prevent the re-emergence of its deep-seated crises (Harvey 2010, 2014). High levels of welfare were already in contradiction with high levels of capital accumulation, a contradiction that the welfare states found they were unable to resolve in any fundamental way.

It is not difficult to understand that the welfare states had sought to mediate the internal antagonism between capital and workers. This resulted in heavy fiscal burdens that made it difficult to continue with welfare state policies. From the neoliberal point of view, high taxes, high welfare spending, and government policies encouraged idleness in the poor and slowed economic growth, creating a burden on government that would ultimately be passed on to capital. At the same time, workers' power was growing, as was their bargaining ability, leading to increases in wages and welfare provision and a corresponding rise in production costs for capital. This meant a reduction in the profit taken by capital. A counter-attack aimed at protecting capital was launched. This is the historical origin of neoliberalism.

Neoliberalism is a rebellion against Keynesian advocacy of state intervention in the economy and the various stripes of social democracy. The economic stance of neoliberalism can be summed up as liberalization of the economy, privatization, marketization, and global integration. Neoliberals have a faith in the infallibility of market self-regulation and believe that a laissez-faire market economy can achieve the best allocation of resources through price adjustments. They believe this to be the most efficient economic system. They are opposed to any kind of state intervention and accuse socialism and planned economies of being "the road to serfdom" (Hayek 2009). They also argue for capital without borders and free trade, and seek to create a "flat earth,"[6] where capital can flow freely worldwide without barriers of any kind.

In 1979 Margaret Thatcher came to power in the UK, then in 1980 Ronald Reagan was elected US President. Neoliberalism moved from being a school of thought to the ideology behind actual power and political and economic policies. Thatcher and Reagan were both extreme in their belief in neoliberal measures. Backed by powerful forces, they implemented domestic privatizations, swingeing welfare cuts, and attacks on the working class and the power of the unions. In Thatcher's view, there was "no alternative"[7] to neoliberalism. Under Anglo-US leadership, the major capitalist nations, including France, Germany, and Italy, made the turn to neoliberalism. At the same time the continually worsening economic crisis intensified class conflict within the capitalist states, forcing capital into a scramble to transfer the crisis to the nations of the Third World.

The Western capitalist states, led by the US, used their political, economic, military, and cultural hegemony to force an entry into the countries of the Third World, promoting neoliberal policies within them and creating the conditions for global expansion of monopoly capital. By investing in developing world ports, airports, and expressways, transnational capital removed the physical barriers to entry into those economies. The power of the various states and international bodies such as the International Monetary Fund, World Bank, and World Trade Organization was also used to introduce neoliberal restructuring – the famous "Washington Consensus" – to debt-ridden Third World nations (Harvey 2010). This cleared the way at an institutional level for the global flow of capital.

At the same time, on the ideological front, the Western nations employed media and educational bodies in a campaign of untrammeled promotion of neoliberalism. US universities trained up a large number of economists from Third World nations, schooling them in the doctrines of neoliberalism. On their return home, these economists, exposed to neoliberal ideology during their education in the US, became important actors on behalf of social elites in domestic economic policy-making, guiding their respective nations toward a neoliberal road.[8]

NEOLIBERALISM AND REFORM IN CHINA

Neoliberalism claims to oppose state intervention, yet paradoxically the spread of the doctrine was achieved only through vigorous and forcible state interventions. Coinciding with the full turn of the global capitalist system to neoliberalism, China made the historic decision to set out on the road of "reform and opening," proactively throwing open wide the nation's doors to global capital; hence, ironically, "reform and opening" in China has been a process of voluntarily embracing global capitalism, remaking the goals of socialist revolution.

The fall of the Gang of Four in 1976 announced the end of China's Cultural Revolution. The ruling party began a process of political transformation, abandoning the political line based on a core of class struggle and shifting the focus of state and party work to economic development. All past errors were deemed to have been due to an "ultra-left line," a line which was thoroughly rejected. In the face of the apparent prosperity of the West, China's ruling elites looked to the West for the country's development. This shift in worldview led to a sudden and profound change in the position China occupied in the world system: from its former place at the forefront of opposition to imperialism and capitalism, China slumped first to a marginal and then rose to a central position in the global capitalist system. Various members of the elite made the long journeys to Europe and America in search of a prescription that might resolve the "problems" China faced. In the universities of the West they came into contact with the neoliberal thinking then prevalent and brought it back to China, where they used it to plan and promote further reforms.

A number of policy decisions concerning reform were made at the Third Full Plenum of the Central Committee of The Eleventh National Party Congress (NPC) in 1978, with China once again taking the path of learning from the West as it had in the last years of the Qing Dynasty. The social elites of the time regarded the US as the most advanced nation in the world and its model of development as the most successful. The most prominent features of this American model were the market, private ownership, and a liberal approach to the economy. The hegemonic discourse created was that the reason China had fallen so far behind the developed nations of the West such as America and was behind even the newly industrialized economies of Southeast Asia was precisely that it did not have a market economy. The socialist model China had followed over the previous 30 years began to be questioned, and severe criticisms were leveled at the planned economy and public ownership at the core of the model. The elite view was that the freedom of labor and entrepreneurs was restricted by the strict controls of the command economy and that this caused a loss of vitality in both economic and social life. The planned economy utilized the household registration system [*hukou*] to maintain the separation of town and country, which created a gap between the two, forming a bipolar rural–urban economic pattern (Cheng and Selden 1994).[9] Public ownership and the collective economy was seen as leading to an egalitarian "eating from the big cooking pot" that lacked any mechanism for rewarding effort and created slack work, idleness, and corruption.

For the neoliberal economists, marketization was the solution to all the many problems China then faced. The market was an invisible hand able to automatically adjust the economy through price mechanisms, allocating resources rationally, achieving the greatest efficiency, and raising productive capacity to its highest possible level. Any intervention in the market would interfere with the normal operation of market mechanisms and would lead to further problems such as corruption. The market could also bring human freedom; the market economy gave full freedom of choice to actors in the market; private ownership, the market, and free trade were more suited to basic human nature (Chen 2008). In sum, the market was raised to the status of a *ne plus ultra* and any doubts concerning it were taken as a sign of thinking that was insufficiently "liberated" or a desire to return to the past, perhaps even leading to being labeled as an "ultra-leftist."

The neoliberal drum-beating for marketization prompted fierce debate in China in the 1980s; Deng Xiaoping brought this to an end with his declaration that there should be "no debate." He set the basic tone for reform: while it was necessary to guard against rightist deviations, the principal task was preventing leftist deviations. Throughout the reform process, economists who believed in neoliberal ideology, under the rubric of "liberated thinking," were active participants in the drafting of policy and played a highly important role. The neoliberal school of thought emanating from Europe and the US became the ideological weapon they employed to assert the legitimacy of reform, and was indeed the guiding ideology of the reform process.

Particularly after the fall of the Soviet Union and the Iron Curtain, socialist praxis suffered a severe setback and the Soviet model was criticized as totalitarian and dictatorial, while in the West scholars loudly pronounced the "end of history" (Fukuyama 2006). Against this background, social elites in China became still firmer in their belief that neoliberalism offered the one true path and was the necessary trend of historical development. In speeches he gave on his "Southern Tour" in 1992, Deng Xiaoping once again affirmed the correctness of China's road to reform. This gave impetus to the progress of reform and opening; a call for the creation of a "socialist market economy" was written into the report of the Fourteenth Party Congress in the same year, establishing the future direction of the reform process.

In brief, over the course of a short three decades, a profound transformation took place in Chinese society. With the support of various preferential policies, vast quantities of foreign capital began to pour into the country. China became a paradise for international investors. In the years between 1979 and 2008, China attracted US$850 billion in direct private foreign investment. Current annual foreign direct investment is some US$80–90 billion, amounting to a sum equivalent to 21 percent of GDP, the highest rate of any developing nation (Gao 2009). More than 480 of the 500 strongest enterprises in the world have invested in China. Massive changes also occurred in the domestic ownership structure of Chinese enterprises, with the state vigorously supporting the development of the non-public or private sector economy. The proportion of GDP generated by the latter grew at a spectacular rate, reaching 60 percent, while the proportion generated in the state-owned sector fell to around a third, retaining its leading role only in the basic industries (Gao 2009). After the layoff and letting go of a large number of workers from state-owned enterprises, individual businesses and private enterprises have become the main source of employment opportunities, which were largely offered to rural migrant workers, accounting for 37.7 percent of employment and more than 90 percent of newly created job opportunities.[10]

There has been a clear increase in the fundamental role of market mechanisms with the price of the vast majority of commodities and services now set by the market. Beginning in the late 1990s, a variety of sectors directly linked to the quality of life of the common people – housing, healthcare, education, etc. – basically became marketized. After marathon talks lasting a dozen years and having paid a very heavy price in concessions made, China finally achieved its goal of accession to the WTO, further raising the level of marketization domestically and openness to external markets. The link-up with the global capitalist system was finally complete.

After 30 years of reform China has been transformed from a global center of revolution for people into a workshop of the world for capital. The commodification of Chinese society has increased very significantly; land, natural resources, labor, and public services have now been commodified. From a planned to a market economy, it is clear that every step of the transformation was the result of intervention by the very visible hand of the state: the invitation of foreign capital investment, the construction of special economic zones and industrial towns for technological development, the provision of high-quality infrastructure, and last but not least, the cheap supply of huge numbers of skilled and educated workforce. In China, the class politics and biopolitics of power were a perfect match, which calls for a new politics of resistance, in which the new laboring subjects will be the major protagonists of social change.

CONCLUSION: THE PATH TO AN URBAN EXPORT-ORIENTED ECONOMIC MODEL

China is now entirely embedded in the neoliberal world, serving as the workshop of the world and making up the world's largest working class.

After 30 years of reform and opening up, fundamental changes have occurred in the structure of China's economy and society and today the country is fully integrated into the global capitalist system and has become the world's second-largest economy. The process of reform and opening up in China took place under the guidance of the state. Neoliberal economists acting as a social elite provided theoretical guidance and specific policy proposals for reform, proposals that were ultimately enacted as actual policy, and were elevated to become the will of the state. A top-down application of state power determined the direction of China's social development and also had a direct impact on the individual members of society in general, and the new working class in particular.

In the reform period the social elite rejected China's former socialist path to development. They were of the view that the socialist system of public ownership could only lead to collective penury and was incapable of achieving economic development and popular prosperity. Guided by Western neoliberalism, China chose an imbalanced development strategy that would give priority to the development of a certain section of the population and certain regions. One concrete manifestation of this was in the industrial structure, with priority given to the development of light industries and the service sector. In terms of regions, it was the coastal provinces of the east that were given priority. In ownership models, growth in the private sector was vigorously promoted; priority was given to urban development rather than rural, in particular the cities in the coastal regions.

During the "reform and opening up" period, guided by the neoliberal economists, a realignment was made in China's path to economic development, adopting an export-oriented economic model and turning China into the workshop of the world. This type of development required a massive amount of labor; the labor requirements of the export-oriented economy combined with the low demand for labor in the small peasant economy to create mutually complementary push and pull factors that set millions upon millions of young rural workers on the one-way road to working as migrants in the cities.

This development strategy based on comparative advantage fashioned a new migrant working class whose labor was cheap and also created a capitalist class in China. Relying on sweatshops and employing every tactic to accumulate primitive capital, this capitalist class rapidly gained in power. At the same time, the state was also obtaining great wealth from rapid economic growth. In 2008 China's fiscal income reached CNY5,000 billion (US$765.5 billion), equivalent to a fifth of total GDP. Yet the price of this export-oriented economic model was that for a long time the interests of the workers were ignored. The state and private enterprise accumulated vast wealth while the workers struggled to escape poverty. Economist Yao Yang calculated that the proportion of GDP going to worker incomes (the sum of both wages and income from self-employment) fell from 60 percent in 1990 to around 48 percent in 2009 (Yao 2009).

Chinese economists believed that this was the only way to create job opportunities for such an enormous labor force and the only way to shift China's population from the countryside to the cities, yet in fact the present development model has signally failed to achieve genuine urbanization. On the one hand, the countryside has been hollowed out of its young labor force; on the other, rural migrants are still locked outside the gates of the cities. In a time when capital has achieved ever more accumulation and the cities have become ever more prosperous, the urban–rural divide has been further widened and peasants are further than ever from genuine urbanization.

In short, over the past 30 years China has created an economic miracle that has caught the attention of the world, especially in the area of alleviation of poverty. Yet this development has come at a heavy price. The dismantling of the collective economy and the state retreat from the countryside meant that agriculture did not develop, rural China remained in poverty, and large numbers of rural people were forced to out-migrate to allow an ample supply of labor for export-oriented industries. Under the export-oriented development model, cheap labor became China's most important competitive advantage.

Faced with the reality of China's increasingly severe problems with agriculture and the countryside, and the urban–rural divide, not only have the neoliberal economists failed to reconsider their economic development model, they have instead blamed the problems on the process of marketization not being thorough enough. In their view the market laws that ensure survival of the fittest can generate the greatest possible incentive mechanisms, and a widening gap between rich and poor must be accepted as a necessary byproduct of the market economy. In this sense, the "free" market does not really exist in the way that most neoliberal economists would hold. Under this actually "unfree" market, equity and effectiveness are an opposed pair that cannot be reconciled. Only if a small proportion of the population is allowed to get rich first can eventual common prosperity be achieved. Only when economic disparities are greatly increased will an incentive mechanism be possible. To this, there is no alternative.

In the face of this phenomenon, we are forced to ask, "Who is paying the price? Who is development for?" These historical debts are soon to be paid by the new laboring subjects. I am compelled to explore these new laboring subjects who are migrant workers, the significant segment of the new Chinese working class that is growing most rapidly; they occupy critical sectors of the economy, and they have become the most militant workers. Moreover, factory and construction workers are the largest, most important, and most militant segments of the migrant workers who form the core of this book.

2 | Capital Meets State: Re-emergence of the Labor Market and Changing Labor Relations

INTRODUCTION

Today China lies squarely within the grid of global capitalism. It is now the capital of capital where all sorts of capital flow continuously into the dreamland of investment and speculation. The rise of China as a major capital of capital, however, is not a natural consequence of the "free" market under the age of globalization as neoliberal economists might assume. In fact, this transformation is ironically state-driven and has been achieved with the collusion of the interests of transnational capital in its search for offshore production relocation in the new age of neoliberal expansion of global capitalism. The temporary defeat of the Cultural Revolution resulted in a reformist party-state that drove forwards the process of "reform and open" policies, bringing globalization into the country and shattering socialist production relations. This state-led process of economic globalization has been accompanied by a state withdrawal from the areas of social reproduction and social protection of the peasantry and working class.

Globalization and market reform have brought profound changes to the mode of production and labor relations in China. First of all, the dismantling of the collective rural economy and the "liberation of labor power" from the collective economy are the prerequisites for the return of capital. Since the 1970s, reformist leaders and business elites have called for the dismantling of the rural collective economy and greater labor flexibility and mobility to reshape China's rural and urban economy under the dictate of a commodity market. After thirty years of huge efforts at socialist transformation in alleviating capitalistic labor relations, labor was now reconsidered as a kind of "commodity" that could be freely exchanged in a nascent market. The free choice for individuals to turn themselves into wage-labor was highly promoted. This call for individual freedom was rendered as "liberating thoughts" from the rigidity of socialist belief so as to open the gates of China to the global economy. This paved the way for re-proletarianization in Marx's sense, as the new laboring subjects now have to turn themselves into "free" subjects, liberated from the collective economy, gradually losing the means of production, having nothing but their labor to sell in a newly recreated labor market. In a sense, everything that could fit into the market economy has to be rebuilt from the sods of socialist soil.

REFORM IN THE COUNTRYSIDE: THE ORIGIN OF NEW LABORING SUBJECTS

Let us review the history of reform and opening in China which paved the way for the creation of the new working class. Reform in China began first in the countryside. In the latter years of the 1970s, the reformist elites were of the view that overall the livelihoods of China's peasantry remained at the low levels of a subsistence economy (Huang 2000 [1992]). The main cause of this situation, they held, was the people's commune system that better suited a larger scale and public ownership: the people's communes tied the peasantry to the land, took away their right and liberty of autonomous economic management, and caused a lack of enthusiasm for production. In the view of the elites, the collective economy was one of low efficiency and went against the laws of economics and the particular features of agriculture. They argued that in the collective economy, peasants "ate from the big pot," fed whether they worked or not, whether they worked hard or not; there were no incentive mechanisms and this restricted the development of rural productive forces (Du 2007: 98). It was for these reasons that the reforming elite vigorously promoted the policy direction of "contracting production to households," namely the household responsibility system.

Many economists believe the household responsibility system was a spontaneous innovation of Chinese peasants. That such innovations were spontaneous in certain areas is not in question; however, the extension of the household responsibility system as the basic economic framework for rural areas nationwide in the reform era was achieved only by the vigorous efforts of the state, and it is in just this sense that we can say that rural reforms embody the neoliberal intent of the reforming elite.

The reality of the household responsibility system was the revival of a petty peasant economy made up of individual families in which the household was the basic economic unit. This was a turning away from the goals of the socialist collective economy and a return to the pre-liberation period of China. Despite the fierce debate, the household responsibility system garnered the approval of high-level central leaders such as Deng Xiaoping. Leaders at all levels were requested to be a little more liberated in their thinking, a little more bold in reforming, and a little more "down-to-earth" in their work (Vogel 2011). In January 1984, the central government extended the land contract period to 15 years, opened up different funding and sales channels, fostered market mechanisms, and gave permission for private individuals to set up businesses. These measures came with the stated aims of promoting growth in rural trade, making rural trade more open, increasing the commodification of the means of production and agricultural produce and overall marketization.

In this manner, the household responsibility system was rapidly put into effect through the promotional efforts of the state. By the early 1980s it was basically in place in most regions nationwide.

Subsequently, the state promulgated a series of policy measures that consolidated the household contracted production responsibility system and stabilized land contract relationships in the countryside. A reform to the constitution was passed at the first plenary session of the Eighth NPC in 1993, adding provisions for the household contracted production responsibility system. Document No. 11 issued in 1997 extended the fixed contracted period for land to 30 years. The disbanding of the people's communes was complete (Vogel 2011).

The early days of reform to the household responsibility system saw quite rapid development of rural productive forces and a large rise in grain production. In 1984 overall grain production exceeded 800 billion jin (400 million tonnes), a historic high and 200 billion jin more than production in 1978. It was this same year that the Chinese government announced to the world that the country had resolved its problems of basic subsistence.[1] At the same time there were also significant production increases in other farm produce, forestry, livestock rearing, sidelines and fisheries, bringing to an end shortages of agricultural produce and also bringing rapid rises in peasant incomes. The policymakers who supported the household responsibility system reforms attributed the entirety of the growth in the agricultural sector to the new contract system. The view among mainstream economists was it was precisely this reform that had brought the Chinese countryside out of poverty and allowed 22 percent of the world's population to be supported on a mere 7 percent of global arable land.

Later, neoliberal economists borrowed some of the concepts of Western institutional economics, in particular theories of property rights, to provide further theoretical justifications for the household responsibility system. After a study visit looking at the effects of China's rural reform, the renowned neoliberal economist Theodore W. Schultz offered his evaluation, that the household responsibility system was the primary motive force in rural social progress. In sum, neoliberal economists placed the blame for all the problems of pre-reform agriculture on collectivization and gave all the credit for the achievements since reform to decollectivization and marketization. As for all the problems that emerged in the countryside after reform, mainstream economists held these to be caused by insufficient marketization and they went on to advocate full privatization of the land (Zhou 2008; Dang and Wu 2014).

In the space of a few short years, the benefits brought by state policy-mandated contracted production began to come to an end. After the bumper grain harvest of 1984, a problem of difficulty selling grain arose in China, with grain prices stagnating for a lengthy period. The rate of growth in rural incomes fell sharply, averaging just 1.7 percent annual growth for the three years between 1989 and 1991, with an actual fall of 0.7 percent in 1990, slumping to a low. At the same time, the great expansion in the gap between urban and rural incomes continued. In 1978 the ratio was 2.5:1, shrinking to 1.7:1 in 1984 then growing to 3.3:1 by 2007.[2]

Of even greater significance was that reform to adopt the household responsibility system was in essence a re-creation of the small peasant economy production model in the Chinese countryside. Although by encouraging enthusiasm in small producers it was able to resolve some of the accumulated problems with the collective economy such as poor management and a lack of incentives, thus achieving a rapid improvement in rural productive forces in a short period of time, yet as the pattern of a market economy guided by capital took shape, the fundamental weakness of the small peasant economy soon became apparent. Due to its small-scale production, the small peasant economy soon proved to be unproductive and uncompetitive in the market. Moreover, the inability of individual family farming to withstand the risks imposed by an external market became apparent. The household responsibility system gave peasants autonomy in the way they ran their farms. In theory they should have been able to decide for themselves what to grow and how much, in the light of market demand, and hence make the best possible earnings. Yet when faced with the extreme fluctuations of the market, small farmers often ended up paying a heavy price. At times when supply of their produce exceeded demand, prices had fallen, and earnings were affected, farmer producers were only able to adjust after the fact, meaning they could only ever lag behind the market. In this sense, it was precisely the household responsibility system reform that created the later predicament of a long-term absence of growth in rural China.

The serious problem was that post-reform, the existing rural collective organizations fell into abeyance. The small peasant production mode of individual household farming meant only low levels of agricultural industrialization. Peasants could only supply the market with primary rural products with little added value. There was little processing of Chinese agricultural produce and so added value was correspondingly low and peasants' earnings were limited. Industrial agriculture requires such means of production as funds, land, and technology; under the individual household mode of production, it was difficult to accumulate sufficient capital to engage in industrial agriculture. The latter was also hard to achieve without the collective economy to rely on.

After accession to the WTO, the domestic agricultural market was opened to an even higher degree. By 2005 the average import tariff on agricultural produce was just 15.35 percent, much lower than that of developed nations such as the US, Japan, or EU states, and lower still than the global average of 62 percent. China's agricultural produce tariffs are among the lowest in the world. Rural produce from overseas came into China with the competitive advantage of high quality and low price. This meant on the one hand a great deal of domestic agricultural produce could not be sold and the prices it earned were too low, and on the other that China relied on imports for much of its agricultural produce. Today, China is the largest importer of US soybeans and cotton. Between 1997 and 2008 China's imports of soybeans rose by 34.56 million tonnes, an average annual growth of 26 percent and accounting for 51.8 percent of the international trade in this commodity. In 2007, imports accounted for 80 percent of China's soya bean consumption.[3]

Indeed, in many inland rural villages, the grain that peasants have expended such bitter efforts to plant rarely produces earnings sufficient to cover costs. The income from farming is now far below the level necessary to cover the consumption demands of rural households. The land that formerly provided home and livelihood to the peasantry now no longer has the status of a means of production, transitioning from being "productive land" to "welfare land."[4] The situation became even more extreme when the earnings from planting crops declined, such that land gradually lost even the ability to function as a source of welfare. Today a great deal of land in rural areas has been abandoned and lies idle. This process represents the gradual loss of the means of production for Chinese peasants.

In sum, a petty peasant economy based on the household unit is by nature an economy geared to self-sufficiency, capable only of resolving the problem of basic subsistence with no prospect of bringing prosperity. Yet rural China today has long since grown far beyond the point where its development can be considered merely in terms of subsistence. As the reforms advanced, the countryside was drawn deeper into the great tide of marketization, and peasant livelihoods became severely dependent on the market and cash incomes. Since the 1990s, the supply of everything from major consumer durables to everyday items like salt, grain, oil, and fuel has become thoroughly marketized. Rural people have become ever more dependent on currency; without cash, even basic subsistence cannot be guaranteed.

Having lost the collective economy that was their foundation, it is no longer possible for the welfare and social security formerly provided by the collective to continue.[5] Now it costs money to send a child to school, it costs money when an older person gets ill – the financial burden on the individual family has increased dramatically. The peasantry, who had resolved the privations of hunger and starvation in the socialist period, now found themselves tightly constrained by the need for money. This is how Old Li, a migrant construction worker from a village in Hebei province in North China describes his family's predicament:

> There's no way the cities could do without us and we've been roped in by the cities. The family has no money, your little one needs to go to school, what can you do about it if you don't go away to work? Everyone in the village from kids who've just left school to fifty-year-olds all go away to work, whole families, just like back in the pre-revolutionary era, doing wage labor for someone else. We support these other people through our work but we only have ourselves to support ourselves.

In the place we visited Old Li, Yao Village in Hebei province, the majority of the young labor force had gone away to work. Out of a village population of 6,000, there were 1,500 people working long-term on construction sites in the cities. Most of the time there simply isn't any chance of making a living staying at home in the village. Old Li has four children, two of whom are at university and two of whom attend high school. Having four children in education makes the financial burden Old Li undertakes particularly heavy. To keep a student at university for a year when you add fees to living expenses costs more than CNY10,000, a sum no ordinary rural family could ever afford if they relied solely on what they earned from farming the land. The only way left to him is to go with his village peers to work on the construction sites as migrant labor.

Neoliberalism attacked the restrictions the planned economy placed on the peasantry and extolled freedom, but the freedom the peasants were given by the neoliberal project was ultimately a handover of themselves to the market. The individual farming family has absolutely no ability to resist the mighty forces of the market. The peasantry who were "liberated" from the collectives scarcely had a moment to enjoy their short-lived freedom before being forced to choose the path of the migrant worker as the price of mere existence in the era of the market economy. They "freely" made their way to the cities and became "free" hired laborers. This sense of alienation, the peasant-workers experienced, started at the gate of the market economy and further carried into the door of the production sphere.

In short, the small peasant economy model provides no way for peasant survival and livelihood in terms of rural production and social reproduction. On the one hand, the petty peasant economy model does not achieve any increase in productivity, on the other, market reforms have led to a precipitous increase in consumer demand. In these circumstances it becomes hard to continue living in the petty peasant economy and rural people are forced to abandon the land and head for the cities to seek another means of earning a living. This is the historical origin of the emergence of the "migrant worker tide," and the creation of the new laboring subjects who underpin China's rise to be the factory of the world.

It was not that the policymakers of rural reform were unaware of the drawbacks of the small peasant economy created under the household responsibility system. Yet in the view of mainstream economists, a vast population could be an important resource for China's industrialization and urbanization. The age structure of the rural population skews to youth, and we are in a time when the bulk of the labor force are in their prime and the dependency burden on households is low. This is the "demographic dividend" population economists speak of with such relish (Cai 2009). These economists hold that since Chinese labor is abundant and cheap, the country must abandon its former path to industrialization that was centered around heavy industry and develop labor-intensive enterprises instead. Only such an approach can absorb an enormous labor force and bring into play China's comparative advantage as a participant in the global division of labor (Lin 2002; Wu 2006).

THE BIRTH OF THE LABOR MARKET

Labor markets re-emerged first in rural areas as township and village enterprises absorbed surplus farm labor following the dismantling of people's communes. With the transformation of labor power into a marketable commodity, the state lifted administrative barriers to both geographical and job mobility while the household registration system continued to control population mobility as well as deprive rural migrant workers of such fundamental rights as pensions and health care. Employment of rural-to-urban migrants in the non-state sector in coastal cities, where welfare benefits are minimal, has grown rapidly since the 1980s. This is the trend that created a new laboring class during the subsequent three decades.

Meanwhile, from the mid-1990s, without the support of the state, township enterprises could hardly compete with the foreign and joint ventures, and the labor force in small and medium state-owned enterprises declined rapidly, with layoffs following enterprise restructuring and privatization. Some of the adversely affected urban workers were able to find jobs in the new economy, while many others were forced into early retirement or informal employment. In the early 2000s, many of the state-owned-enterprise workers became jobless, and if they were lucky enough to find a job, they became temporary workers in an increasingly unstable market. The socialist class workforce was seriously damaged when the majority of state workers became temporary or precarious workers, having their lives deeply dependent on the logics of the market. The mastery of the revolutionary state workers, who were entitled to lifetime benefits in exchange for their political loyalty to the party, has faded since the demise of Maoism. Thus the new Chinese working class has been drastically remade under the state-led policies of agricultural reform, industrial privatization, and export processing.

This state-in process of globalization has created a new millions-strong working class in China. A paradoxical phenomenon is that when we see this state-in process in economic globalization, it is accompanied by a state-out process, in which the state has radically retreated from the areas of social reproduction and social protection. This chapter looks at this paradox of state-in and state-out processes of globalization and how it has shaped the new working class in China. An interesting observation is that while the contemporary Chinese state looks schizoid, it is because when the reformist state meets capital, it has already abandoned its representation of the interests of the peasantry and working class, as it works boldly and hastily to serve the interests of capital, including transnational capital. This is the victory of neoliberal global capitalism over the socialist China under the auspices of the state, which nature and social representation has shifted and remade since the end of the Cultural Revolution.

Two events illustrate the change in nature of the Chinese state and its role in transforming its economy, that is, the establishment of the Special Economic Zones (SEZs) in the 1980s and entry into the WTO in 2001. The establishment of SEZs signified the opening of China's urban economy to export-industrial development, a departure from the socialist economy that had been the bedrock of the Chinese revolution. China's entry into the WTO further signaled a complete incorporation of China's economy into the arena of global capitalism, and China became a central part of it. These two events were launched by the ruling power with determined will, despite internal disagreements within the party and the society at large.

First of all, four SEZs were set up in coastal China, signifying a farewell to its socialist planned economy and a reunion with a flexible global market economy. In 1980 Shenzhen, the first SEZ, was erected as a window to attract foreign investment via Hong Kong and later

Taiwan, Korea, and Japan. In 1992, Deng Xiaoping staged the "Southern Tour" to the Shenzhen SEZ and Guangdong province, stimulating a new wave of foreign investment. Industrial zones, factory compounds, workers' dormitories, and other facilities were built and supported by governmental infrastructure projects such as airports, highways, power stations, customs houses, etc. Privileged policies and measures such as exemption from taxes, free provision of industrial land (or at very low prices), and facilitation of labor supplies were provided to serve the transborder or transnational capital. All of these were carried out by a self-proclaimed socialist state, with the aim of gaining ground in the grid of the global economy.

The reformist state made huge efforts to bring the country into the WTO, providing a further driving force for economic globalization in the twenty-first century. After more than ten years of negotiation, China 'won' its membership of the WTO on December 11, 2001. It had very significant implications for China's export and investment activities. Taking the garment and textile industry as an example, it is the active role of government to shape and reshape the transformation of the industry. On January 1, 2005, the Multi-Fibre Agreement (MFA), which had limited China's export of garment products, was eventually phased out among WTO members. After the phasing-out of the MFA, China further signed bilateral Free Trade Agreements (FTAs) with countries such as Thailand, Pakistan and Chile, as well as the Closer Economic Partnership Arrangement (CEPA) with Hong Kong SAR. Negotiations on more FTAs with other countries (including India, New Zealand, and Singapore) are ongoing. Among these, significant progress has been achieved with the ASEAN countries (the Association of Southeast Asian Nations). Shortly after this historical change in the international trade regime in which the Chinese government was actively involved, China emerged to be the biggest garment exporter in 2004 with 26.6 percent of the world's total exports; if Hong Kong is taken into account, the proportion was as high as 38 percent.

In the same year, the textile and clothing industries in China employed 19 million workers or 18.9 percent of the total workforce in the country's manufacturing sectors.

To serve the needs of capital, the development of the SEZs and technology development zones across China, similar to the development of corresponding establishments in most other developing economies, was based on a massive harnessing of young workers, in particular of unmarried women, who are often the cheapest and most compliant labor (see Lee 1998; Pun 1999, 2005). The government at different levels partially relaxed the household registration system and actively coordinated the transfer of the "surplus labor" to the booming cities. By the mid-1990s, rural surveys estimated that the number of internal migrant laborers ranged between 50 and 70 million nationwide (Gaetano and Jacka 2004). In 2014, the size of the migrant working population was over 270 million, spread all over the country and occupying all industry sectors.[6]

The Chinese state has taken a very active role in promoting massive rural-to-urban labor migration and creating a new labor market to serve the export-oriented industrialization over the past three decades. Owing to the deep rural and urban divide highly shaped by neoliberal development strategies, rural authorities have submitted to the central government's direction by exploring inter-provincial labor cooperation and coordination program initiatives, bringing about rapid labor mobility for urban economic growth. From the 1990s onwards, the provinces of Hunan, Hubei, Jiangxi, Sichuan, and Anhui, to name just a few, have systematically exported their rural labor to Guangdong in the South. In exchange, these interior provinces have benefited from the remittances sent back by rural migrant workers. This migration policy also assures a continuous replenishment of internal migrant laborers to the production powerbases in the coastal cities. Strong state initiatives support the labor needs of emerging industries and facilitate labor supply flow to the manufacturing sites (Pun et al. 2010). Many local governments from various provinces set up labor management offices in Shenzhen to facilitate the supply of migrant youth into the foreign-invested factories. Factories in different industrial zones of Shenzhen were centrally connected to different counties and townships in inland provinces of China, which had to provide a designated amount of labor to work in these foreign-invested factories.

In this sense, the labor market was deliberately created by the Chinese state, which used its administrative power to turn the "socialist peasants" into "capitalist commodities" for the benefit of capital use. The government's labor management offices served as the agency in the market: they first screened and recruited young people, especially women, and then transferred them directly to the factories in the industrial regions. The arrangements made by these labor offices were sometimes very detailed, such as arranging long distance coaches to transport rural women to work, in return for management fees per head from the company.

NEW LABORING SUBJECTS AND WORKERS' WAGES

In reformed China, a new labor market has been created politically to facilitate the exchanges of new laboring subjects as labor commodities. These peasant-workers are often called *dagongmei/zai*, laboring girls and boys, which is a new gendered labor subject, produced at the particular moment when private and transnational capital came to China. As a newly coined term, *dagongmei/zai*, embraces multi-layered meanings denoting a new kind of labor relationship fundamentally different from that of Mao's period. *Da-gong* (laboring) means "working for the boss" or "selling labor," connoting commodification and a capitalist exchange of labor for wages. It is a new concept that stands in contradiction to Chinese socialist history. Labor, especially alienated wage labor, supposedly emancipated with the Chinese revolution, is again sold to the capitalists, and this time under the auspices of the state. In contrast to the term *gongren*, state worker, which carried the highest status in the socialist rhetoric of Mao's day, the new word *dagong* signifies a lesser status – that of a hired hand – in a new context shaped by the rise of market factors in labor relations and hierarchy (Pun 2005).

Looking from the laboring subjects' point of view, there is a huge desire to out-migrate from the countryside. Young rural men and women alike find no way to compete with the low prices for agricultural products in the post-WTO accession era. Together with limited educational opportunities, and limited village employment opportunities – indeed, these last two challenges are particularly intolerable for younger generations who grew up in the reform period – the rural youth have no choice but to go to work at 16 or 17 years of age. Some rural women also aspire to escape arranged marriages, familial conflicts, and patriarchal relations. Still others want to widen their horizons and to experience modern life and cosmopolitan consumption in the cities. Indeed, personal pursuit of out-migration – shaped by the state-led export-oriented development strategy – fits with the goal of the state in channeling labor migration from rural to coastal industrial areas.

Ironically, the creation of a new labor market largely by the Chinese state for global capital accumulation was accompanied by a process of state withdrawal from the areas of social reproduction and social protection, especially in the rural communities. The household registration system (*hukou*) was often criticized as an unreasonable barrier that created severe discrimination against rural migrants to work and live in the city. In reality, the household registration system was seriously manipulated by capital and local state to create exploitative mechanisms of labor appropriation in the increasingly competitive world. This is the state-out process of globalization: China's globalized economy needs the labor of the rural population but does not need the city-based survival of that population once market demand for rural-to-urban migrants' labor power shifts in either location or industry. This newly forming working class is permitted to form no permanent roots and legal identities in the city. Still worse, the *hukou* system, integrated with its labor mechanism, constructs the ambiguous identity of rural migrant labor and simultaneously deepens and obscures the exploitation of this huge laboring workforce. Hence, this subtle and multi-faceted marginalization of rural labor has created a contested, if not a deformed, citizenship, which has greatly disadvantaged Chinese migrant workers who attempt to transform themselves into urban workers.

Being extraordinarily dislocated in the cities, migrant labor is distinguished by its transient nature. A worker, especially a female worker, will usually spend a number of years working as a wage laborer in an industrial city before getting married. Upon marriage, most of the women have to return home because of the difficulty of setting up their family in the city. Rural communities have long exercised – and have long been expected to exercise – the extended planning of life activities such as marriage, procreation, and family. The reproduction of labor of the next generation is hence left to the rural villages, which bear the cost of industrial development in urban areas, even though the ability of the rural communities to take up the reproduction costs is very doubtful. Worse still, physical or mental rehabilitation in the case of serious industrial injuries and occupational diseases are presumed to be taken care of in their rural homes.

This ends up as a process of unfinished proletarianization of Chinese labor, which is driven by the state but at the same time crippled by it. Traumatically hurt, one of the most pressing issues is the suppression of wages for the entire newly formed working class. The official categorization of peasant workers – wage laborers of rural household registration – keeps their social status and class identities ambiguous. Hence, the wage that a migrant receives from working in the factory is not for supporting their livelihood in the city, but it is presumed that the costs of social reproduction of the workers is absorbed in the rural communities. This means that their family, marriage, procreation, childrearing, and retirement are taken care of in the original rural location from which they migrated. Hence, the unfinished process of proletarianization of rural labor enabled a production regime within which a separation exists between the production sphere in the industrial regions and social reproduction in the rural areas (Pun and Lu 2010a). The wages the whole migrant working class earns are much lower than the average costs of social reproduction of labor in the place where they work. In short, the salary they receive is not for them to live in the industrial cities but to prepare them for return to their rural homelands.

This structural factor directly affected how the minimum wage was set in China. The concept of a minimum wage is far more important in China than in other industrialized countries because it affects almost every migrant worker. Unlike other Western countries, the minimum wage is used to protect around ten percent of the workforce, preventing their income from falling below poverty levels. In China, the minimum wage adversely set the wage standard for almost all migrant workers. For instance, Foxconn, up to May 2010 – the high tide of workers' suicides – had never raised basic wages above the local statutory minimum levels for entry-level workers. In June 2010, under public pressure, Foxconn increased the basic wage for workers in its Shenzhen facilities from 900 yuan to 1,200 yuan per month (from US$142 to US$189). It offered them a higher wage "for their hearts," commented China Central Television.[7] It was a rare instance in which the company paid basic wages above the statutory minimum wage, but only barely. Foxconn's wage rate was 9 percent higher than the minimum city-level wage of 1,100 yuan/month (US$173), which took effect on July 1, 2010.

Under the decentralization policy and the 1993 Regulation on Enterprise Minimum Wages, local governments are given the autonomy to formulate their own level of legal minimum wage. Minimum wage levels in each province, municipality, and autonomous region are set in light of local conditions of poverty. Shenzhen, the Greater Shanghai area and coastal cities report higher minimum wage levels than the northern, central, and western regions. As of June 2012, Shenzhen (US$236/month) and Shanghai (US$228/month) had the highest minimum wages, while Chengdu and Chongqing barely surpassed the 1,000 yuan benchmark (US$165/month). Of the 12 surveyed cities where Foxconn has factories, labor in interior cities cost about one-fourth to one-third that in the largest coastal metropolises (see table 2.1). The Chengdu and Chongqing complexes with the two lowest minimum wages in 2012 were among those built in the wake of the 2010 suicides, as Foxconn sought to transfer workers out of high minimum-wage areas such as Shenzhen and Shanghai where its workforce had previously been concentrated.

The 2011 All-China Federation of Trade Unions (ACFTU) survey shows that young migrant workers (those who were born after 1980) earned 1,747.87 yuan per month on average (US$275), compared with the 3,046.61 yuan per month on average (US$479) earned by laborers with permanent urban resident permits, that is, only 57.4 percent of the latter.[8] One factor is crucial in differentiating the incomes of rural migrants and urban-registered workers: in most cities, migrants are not provided with social security, and even those who are so provided find it difficult to carry their benefits to new localities when they change jobs.[9] By law, employers should provide five types of social insurance and one housing fund: old age pensions, medical insurance, unemployment benefits, work-injury insurance, and maternity insurance, plus a mandatory housing provident fund.[10] This is an occupation-based welfare system (that is, employer and employee contributions), alongside welfare provisions by the state or private companies. But rural migrant workers, who cannot carry their retirement benefits with them, are at a severe disadvantage compared with their fellow workers

Table 2.1: Minimum wage requirements in the 12 surveyed cities, 2010, 2012, and 2014

	DECEMBER 2010	JUNE 2012	JULY 2014
	YUAN	YUAN	YUAN
Shenzhen, Guangdong Province	1,100	1,500	1,808
Shanghai	1,120	1,450	1,820
Kunshan, Jiangsu Province	960	1,320	1,530
Nanjing, Jiangsu Province	960	1,320	1,480
Hangzhou, Zhejiang Province	960	1,310	1,470
Tianjin	920	1,310	1,680
Taiyuan, Shanxi Province	850	1,125	1,450
Langfang, Hebei Province	900	1,100	1,480
Wuhan, Hubei Province	900	1,100	1,300
Zhengzhou, Henan Province	800	1,080	1,240
Chengdu, Sichuan Province	850	1,050	1,400
Chongqing	680	1,050	1,250

Source: China's Human Resources and Social Security Bureau.

who enjoy urban residence. This is another reason for the difficulty in earning a living wage in the city for the migrants.

MADE IN CHINA

Hence, the "China price" of export goods as being globally competitive was fundamentally built upon the creation of a massive new laboring class, which until recent years has been paid at the local minimum wage

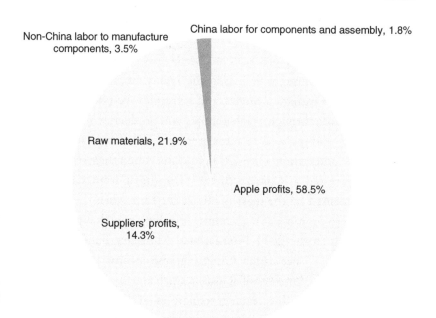

Figure 2.1: Distribution of the value in an iPhone, 2010
Source: based on Kraemer et al. (2011: 5).

levels. The extraordinary amount of surplus value produced by this new working class was taken away mainly by the transnational corporations and their suppliers. For instance, look at the distribution of value for an iPhone which Chinese workers toil day and night to manufacture (figure 2.1).

Apple's strength is well illustrated by its ability to capture an extraordinary 58.5 percent of the value of the iPhone despite the fact that manufacture of the product was entirely outsourced. Particularly notable was that labor costs in China accounted for the smallest share, only 1.8 percent, or nearly US$10, of the US$549 retail price of the iPhone in 2010. Other major component providers, mainly Japanese and South Korean firms that produce the most sophisticated components, captured slightly over 14 percent of the value of the iPhone. The cost of raw materials was just over one-fifth of the total value (21.9 percent).

The labeling of the products as "Made in China" thus creates a misleading impression, as it masks the reality of the transnational corporate power eating up profits, and subsumes the phenomenon of labor exploitation through a global supply and production chain. Often the label was manipulated to misrepresent a global capital war in a nation-state competition when US politicians voiced their criticism of China and created a "Chinese threat." The threat from China was usually augmented by the mass media at the time when the Chinese elites sought to promote a "big" country, excelling in global politics. In fact, according to the 2011 International Monetary Fund's country data on (nominal) per capita GDP, Chinese income did not rank among the world's lowest, but it was a small fraction of that of the developed countries. The leading economies of East Asia revealed wide differences in per capita incomes: Singapore ranked 13th in the world (US$49,271), Japan 18th (US$45,920), South Korea 35th (US$22,411) and Taiwan 39th (US$20,101).[11] At the other end of the spectrum, however, China had per capita GDP of US$5,414 (ranked 88th following the Dominican Republic and just ahead of Jamaica), Indonesia US$3,509 (ranked 110th) and Vietnam US$1,374 (ranked 141st).[12] These modest per capita incomes and their corollary, large portions of the new laboring class living in dire poverty, are indicative of the limits of economic growth that has been so widely celebrated, yet produced such divergent results across the nations of East and Southeast Asia (Pun et al. forthcoming). "Made in China," a label that misrepresented the wealth distribution in the global production chain, placed China in an astonishing position in the global economy.

The label "Made in China" was also misleading in that it disguised huge class cleavages and social inequalities in society at large. Although China's National Bureau of Statistics prudently ceased reporting the country's Gini coefficient after 2000, other statistics show that average rural migrant workers continue as low-wage earners among urban dwellers. Throughout the 1990s and 2000s, the statutory minimum wage standards were often the maximum pay rates for rural migrant workers.[13] With rising food prices and general living costs between 2006 and 2010, provincial-level governments raised local minimum wages by an average of 12.5 percent annually, except for a wage freeze in 2009 during the economic recession.[14] In 2009, the average monthly wage of China's migrant workers was 1,417 yuan (US$223), including overtime premiums.[15] When we turn to the high end of the spectrum, in 2010 China had 960,000 millionaires (one person in every 1,400) and 60,000 people who possessed more than 10 million yuan (US$1.5 million) in personal wealth, a 9.7 percent increase over the previous year. In 2014 there were 152 Chinese billionaires by *Forbes'* reckoning.[16]

CONCLUSION

Global capitalism has won a victory in incorporating socialist regimes into its process of capital accumulation in the last century. With the advent of capital into China's export processing zones in the early 1980s, the country has been greatly transformed into a market economy. This transformation is mostly state driven and has colluded with the interests of transnational capital in its need for offshore production relocation. The launch of Deng Xiaoping's reforms and open polices in 1978 was historic and unprecedented. It changed not only the path of Chinese socialism but also the road of global capitalism. The Chinese state has brought the country into the WTO, further demonstrating this state-in process of economic globalization.

Today, the mode of production and capital-labor relationship in China has been entirely reshaped under the dictates of the global market. The rapid expansion of export-oriented production has led to a sharp rise in jobs in private, foreign-owned, and joint venture enterprises that are now spread over all the cities and towns of China. Since the late 1970s, the de-collectivization project has generated a massive labor surplus from rural areas. At the same time, the central government has created a new labor market by facilitating an unprecedented surge in internal rural-to-urban migration by partially loosening the restrictions on the household registration system. Most transnational corporations (TNCs) or their subcontractors recruit millions of these rural migrants in export-oriented industrial zones as wage-laborers and as disposable commodities.

The socialist legacy of contracting agricultural lands to individual rural households is one of the enabling factors for China to achieve phenomenal economic growth: employers do not need to pay their peasant-workers a living wage or the full cost of social reproduction of labor, which are supposed to be subsidized by the workers' rural communities. Local host governments likewise have shunned their responsibility to improve the livelihood of internal migrant workers and their families under their jurisdiction. This state-out process largely shapes a specific capital–labor relationship, which has contributed to a growing number of struggles for migrant workers in China.

In sum, this state-in and state-out paradoxical process of globalization has resulted in the formation of a new working class in China which is left unprotected in the new labor market. Alongside the rise of a new working class in the industrial and urban areas, the state at various levels is almost missing in providing collective services such as housing, education, medical care, and other basic necessities for migrant workers, in particular, to live in the towns and cities. This has been the foundation for the path to proletarianization of Chinese peasant-workers.

<table>
<tr><td>

3

</td><td>

Building China: Struggle
of Construction Workers

_____

</td></tr>
</table>

A global China is only spatially made possible by construction workers. This chapter looks at the lived experiences of construction workers who are often the "invisible subjects," overlooked, if not entirely neglected, by existing labor studies. The glamorous skylines of Shanghai and Beijing today seem to crystallize Chinese dreams of modernity and global status. These modern cityscapes, however, are underpinned by a construction industry composed of close to 60,000,000 peasant-workers hailing from all parts of the Chinese countryside. I spent more than eight years since 2007 working with a research and service team made up mainly of scholars and students from Beijing. Policy studies, participation observation, and action research were the major methods we explored. We visited construction workers not only at the construction sites in cities such as Beijing, Shanghai, Shenzhen, and Guangzhou, but also followed them back to their home towns in Henan, Hebei, and Zhejiang provinces mostly at Spring Festival time. A supporting network among construction workers and student volunteers has been built, and more than 3,000 construction workers have joined it, of which a few hundred have either suffered industrial accidents or occupational risks, and many more have experiences of collective action.

The rapid development of the construction industry has enabled a highly exploitative labor subcontracting system to emerge. This labor system includes two processes: the rapid commodification of labor through non-industrial social relations organized by a quasi-labor market in the rural villages; and the expropriation of labor during the construction sector production process in urban areas. These two processes shape a labor subcontracting system that is specific to reform-era China, resulting in a never-ending process of wage arrears and the struggle of construction workers to pursue delayed wages in various ways, often involving violent collective action.

Almost no other industry has experienced a boom comparable to construction.[1] The Chinese construction industry has been consuming half of the world's concrete and a third of its steel and employs about 60 million people, most of them rural workers coming from all over the country. About 22.3 percent of all migrant workers from the countryside work in the industry.[2] In order to build Beijing and Shanghai into China's global cities and speed up the process of urbanization, since the Tenth Five-Year Plan (2001–05) China has invested about 376 billion yuan in construction each year. Construction is now the fourth-largest industry in the country. At the turn of the twenty-first century, this industry accounted for 6.6 percent of China's GDP; by the end of 2007, its total income had risen by 25.9 percent to 5.1 trillion yuan, and gross profits had risen 42.2 percent to 156 billion yuan.[3] The total industrial output value of China's construction and building material industry was US$1,873 billion in 2011, 22.6 percent higher than in 2010. As shown in figure 3.1,[4] there has been rapid growth of total industrial output since 2007, and no indication of any effects of the global financial crisis in 2008.

Despite the enormous gross profits and output value of the construction industry, construction workers are poorly protected as regards physical and financial risks, compared to most other workers.[5] The working lives of construction workers are also deeply affected by quarrels, individual and collective fighting, attempts to damage buildings, bodily abuse, and even suicidal behavior. At construction sites, we observed a variety of violent actions taken by construction workers which were no doubt caused by the political economy of the construction industry.

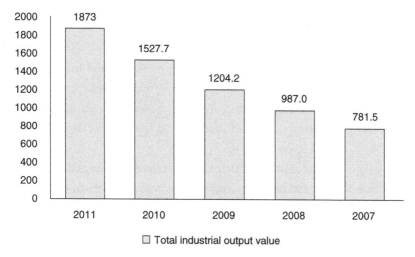

Figure 3.1: Total industrial output of China's construction and building materials industry, 2007–2011 (US$bn)
Source: China Building Material Industry Association.

THE PAST AND THE PRESENT

"No urban youth are willing to work on the construction site. Don't look at me right now. After work and after bathing, I'll look completely different and have a new face", said a 20-year-old Hebei man, covered with dust and dirt, who felt ashamed of being a construction worker. These feelings reflect a notorious image of chronic wage arrears, heavy casualties, and labor conflicts over unpaid wages in the industry.

In nineteenth-century China, construction craftsmen were recruited from renowned "cradles of building craftsmen" in Hebei, Jiangsu, and Shandong to help build urban centers.[6] Such craftsmen were considered to be masters or skilled labor, and enjoyed relatively high social status compared to farmers or small businessmen. New laborers came to learn from masters through apprenticeship (Hershatter 1986). The construction craftsmen were organized through a guild system which provided professional protection and a monopoly over the industry. As the historian Lynda Shaffer put it,

> The fundamental goal of the guild was to present a solid front to a potentially hostile world…In order to ensure that their own numbers expanded no more rapidly than the local market, they placed strict limits on the number of apprentices that could be accepted. (1978: 381)

The original and dominant relationship between master and journeyman was that of teacher and student, so conflicts between employer and employee were not as sharp as those seen in the modern factory or labor subcontracting system (Shaffer 1978: 383). Hence, construction workers in pre-Republic China had their own associational power to protect their labor rights, unlike those of today's China.

In the middle of the nineteenth century, Western construction companies arrived in China and began to recruit rural workers through a labor subcontracting system to be wage laborers in construction projects. After 1880, Chinese companies also initiated such a system. These actions undermined the guild system. Some masters became entrepreneurs, and stopped working as carpenters or masons. Only their employees, the journeymen, still performed manual labor.[7] The journeymen soon found that they were proletarians, lacking the support of their guilds. This is the historical root of Mao's leadership of the 4,000 construction workers who went on strike and founded the Changsha Construction Workers' Union in 1922.

In the early days of the PRC, the Chinese Communist Party (CCP) government relied on construction workers to rebuild ruined cities and war-torn communities in both urban and rural areas. A shortage of construction workers led the State Council to utilize labor from the People's Liberation Army, and in 1952 eight army divisions were turned into state-owned construction enterprises. Labor subcontracting persisted.

In 1958, the labor subcontracting system was ended. Construction work was organized under state-owned or collective enterprises. Workers in urban or rural collectives generally received less protection and fewer benefits than workers in state-owned enterprises (SOEs), but their food was provided and they enjoyed modest but regular payments and reasonable working hours. During this period, construction jobs were viewed as skilled and respected work, and construction workers were often propagandized as "model workers" contributing to the rebuilding of the socialist country. Being pulled from a rural collective to work in the construction industry was a positive experience. A 60-year-old construction master from a village in Tang County, Hebei Province, told us,

> We had to pay the production brigade [that is, their village] 1 yuan every day we left to work for a construction team in the 1970s and 1980s. At that time, there were few subcontractors, and also few cases of cheating. We all got paid after we finished the work. The work team usually provided us with work uniforms, hard hats, work boots and other daily necessities. Nowadays, the subcontractors are different. They all cheat people. We were fine in our time and we were seldom cheated.

By 1980, the number of employees in state-owned construction enterprises was 4.82 million, while the workforce in urban construction collectives numbered 1.66 million and those in rural collectives 3.34 million. Fewer than 10,000 employees worked at privately owned construction enterprises.[8]

THE EMERGENCE OF THE LABOR SUBCONTRACTING SYSTEM

The Deng-era reforms brought an abrupt end to socialist labor practices in the construction industry. In 1978, Deng Xiaoping pointed out that construction could be a profit-making industry. The reform objectives set for the construction industry included restructuring the industry's administrative system, opening construction markets, allowing autonomy in SOEs, establishing a competitive bidding system, and improving project managerial skills (Mayo and Liu 1995). In 1980, a World Bank project, Lubuge Hydropower in Yunnan Province, challenged socialist practices in the construction sector by adopting international competitive bidding for its work. The practice of bidding and the subcontracting system in the construction industry re-emerged (Guang 2005).

In 1984, the State Council issued a document stating: "The state-owned construction and installation enterprises shall reduce the number of permanent workers gradually. In future they shall not, in principle, recruit any permanent workers except skilled operatives necessary to keep the enterprise technically operational."[9] Another significant 1984 regulation, the "Separation of Management from Field Operations," stated that general contractors or contracting companies should not directly employ their blue-collar workforce.[10] Rather, they should employ labor subcontractors who were to be responsible for recruiting the workforce. These regulations accelerated change in the management of the construction industry and the composition of its workforce, leading to today's problems. Driven by state initiatives, construction enterprises were further marketized and field operations were delinked from direct management through the labor subcontracting system.

By the late 1990s, the restructuring of the construction industry was almost complete.[11] While it is arguable that this series of dramatic changes increased efficiency and productivity in the operation of construction projects, a direct result was the emergence of a multi-tier labor subcontracting system. Millions of workers are today part of this labor contracting system, organized through subcontractors who recruit teams of migrant workers from rural areas.[12]

In the actual operation of the industry, there has been a delinking of capital from industry, and of management from labor. In the production chain, top-tier contractors control construction projects through their relationships with property developers and the local state but outsource their work to low-tier subcontractors. The top-tier contractors seek to make a profit by transferring investment risks and labor recruitment to their subcontractors. "They don't bother to get their hands dirty. They transfer all the risks to us. They make us face the workers at times of wage arrears when the money doesn't arrive from above," said Lao Feng, a third-tier subcontractor who, like many others, complained about the top-tier contractors.

We may take a construction project in a Beijing migrant community as an example (see figure 3.2). The subcontracting system began with a well-known property developer who was responsible for land reclamation and the design of a villa project. Responsibility for the construction was shifted down the chain through a bidding process to a state-owned construction company, which only took charge of the project management and equipment arrangement for its contractors. In turn, this company relied on three "big contractors" (*dabao*) who came from Jiangsu, Hebei, and Guangdong; these were responsible for providing raw materials and labor for the project. Two of them set up a labor service company to help recruit rural laborers, but in reality they relied on labor-supplier subcontractors (*xiaobao* or *qingbao*) to recruit the labor, manage the daily division of work, and pay out wages on completion of the project. In return, these labor-supplier subcontractors further depended on labor-use facilitators (*daigong*), usually relatives or co-villagers, to look for workers in their own or surrounding villages. Thus, for this building project, 1,000 workers were organized into a number of small subcontracting teams that worked on the construction site. The number of workers in each subcontracting team ranged from a dozen to 100.

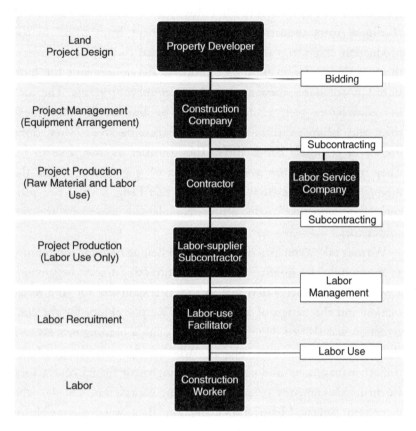

Figure 3.2: The subcontracting system of the construction industry

Most contractors and subcontractors do not have capital to spare, and most of them also operate without access to a credit facility. About half of the construction projects lack adequate funding at the time of budget approval, and triangular debts in the construction industry account for a large portion of China's total triangular debt.[13] Inasmuch as the developers at the top of the pyramid do not make the bulk of their payments to the contractors until the project is completed, the labor subcontractors in turn often face a shortage of available funds even at an early stage of building. The workers have had to become accustomed to a system in which they themselves do not receive their salary until the project is completed and the contractors and subcontractors have been paid.

The construction projects that we studied in Beijing made very low profits for the subcontractors, who often did not have sufficient funds to tide them over until their final payment. In one instance, the work was the construction of 108 villas of 300–500 square meters. Lao Feng, an experienced subcontractor, provided us with detailed information: to build a block of villas estimated to sell for about 10 million yuan, the bidding price was only 760,000 yuan (including the costs of raw materials, labor, and administration) for the first-tier contractors, who further outsourced the construction work to a second tier of contractors, who further subcontracted the work to labor-supplier subcontractors. The standard unit price set for labor costs was 80,000 yuan per villa, which meant that the third-tier and fourth-tier labor-supplier subcontractors had only this lump sum from which to pay the workers they recruited and from which to still make a profit. Lao Feng explained, "We almost lost money in building the villas.[14] Sometimes we run into debts but we still have to keep ourselves in the production chain, otherwise we will be left out." What Lao Feng hoped for was the opportunity to contract the interior renovation jobs after the villas had been sold. As he explained, "When the rich buy a 10-million villa, they use an additional 1 million for renovation. I am waiting to try my luck to get that work."

Taking on a money-losing project with a view to compensating for the initial loss by getting an inside track on the new homeowner's interior renovations was the business logic of the low-tier subcontractors. Coming from places like Hebei, Anhui, Sichuan, and Shandong, most of the contractors and subcontractors had little bargaining power with the construction companies, which were mainly from big cities like Beijing and Guangzhou and were often transformed SOEs with good connections with the city government. The contractors and labor subcontractors often faced serious arrears even in the modest payments owed to them during the early stages of construction, and they were in a weak position when facing the locally influential developers and construction companies. As in almost every other industrial sector in China, the local state thus teams up with capital (whether private or state-owned) to shift risk and to exploit migrant workers from other parts of the country, and wage arrears have consequently become a chronic phenomenon. Over-speculation, insufficient project funding and the absence of state oversight of the industry are also factors. More than anything else, however, the labor subcontracting system, which delinks capital from industry and management from labor, creates a power imbalance in the production chain, to the advantage of the top-tier contractors.

THE EXPROPRIATION OF LABOR IN THE PRODUCTION PROCESS

Accompanying China's rapid urban and industrial development and the further expansion of the construction industry in the 1990s was a tremendous demand for cheap labor. The provision of this labor through the subcontracting system has been a joint creation of capitalist firms and the state. The state changed management–labor relations in the industry, ordering the construction industry to rely upon subcontracting and turning SOEs into profit-making corporations. Local government, sometimes in defiance of laws passed by the central state, also favors first-tier contractors over lower-tier contractors in disputes. Firms are all too happy to manipulate and profit from this arrangement.

In the late 1990s the labor subcontracting system matured, leaving the rural workforce entirely without state or social protection. They had no health cover, no insurance to cover accidents, and no injury payments. By the end of the 1990s, subcontractors recruited rural workers as casual laborers, and did not even provide their workers with a legal contract as required by the Labor Law of 1995. Up to the present, none of the construction workers whom we interviewed had received regular monthly payments, and none had signed a labor contract. Despite the fact that the new Labor Contract Law was in force as of January 2008, neither the contractors nor subcontractors observed it, and most workers were unaware of the new legal obligations placed on their contractors. When we asked workers, the usual answer was: "What's a labor contract? No, we don't have it. I never heard of it."

Most of the workers we interviewed in Beijing from December 2012 to July 2014 had been promised a daily pay rate ranging from 150 yuan to 200 yuan, depending on the type of job and the skills required. However, they were often ultimately paid at a substantially lower rate, and were even at risk of never receiving any payments at all. Without contracts, they have very limited grounds for pursuing their employers through the courts.

Instead of payouts of a weekly or monthly wage, construction workers are usually paid an irregular living allowance arranged by their subcontractors, until the completion of the project or at the end of the year. The allowance ranges from a hundred to a few hundred yuan per month (about 10–20 percent of their promised monthly income), depending on the subcontractor – barely enough to cover food and other daily expenses. Of the subcontractors whom we interviewed, Mr Song was the most sympathetic to his workers:

> If the workers followed you, but they had no money to spend, or if a worker caught the flu and had no money to buy medicines, you had to give them one or two hundred yuan.

Many subcontractors had to use their own money to provide a living allowance to their workers. Some of the workers received no living allowance at all, because their subcontractor claimed to have no money. Significant extraction of labor value in the production process was made possible when wages were replaced by living allowances and when subcontractors justified this practice by saying that there were no funds for salaries coming from their contractor.

We often visited the construction workers in their dormitory at a construction site. A 50-year-old Hubei worker showed us a notepad with all the details of his daily work, saying,

> We're not even workers. Workers sell their labor to the boss and in return they get their wage … As construction workers, we are different. I have been working 286 days for the boss and I still can't get my pay. I'm waiting for my working money (*gongqian*),[15] just as I'm always waiting for my luck.

Because of the promise of a relatively high wage compared to jobs in manufacturing or service industries, many migrant workers are willing to work in the construction sector despite the problem of wage arrears.[16] In addition, male construction workers who have reached the age of 50 have few other job options.

THE COMMODIFICATION OF LABOR THROUGH NON-INDUSTRIAL SOCIAL RELATIONS

Rapidly changing social relations in rural areas have further complicated the problems and conflicts arising from the labor subcontracting system, which originally operated through kin, ethnic, and hometown networks. At the village research site in Hebei, most households derived income from construction work. It was not a particularly poor village, with annual family incomes in the range of 15,000–20,000 yuan. We visited more than 30 families with one or more members working on construction sites in Beijing. Most of these families had both father and son working in the sector. These families were keen to show us the "debt papers" that they had collected in the past years, each telling a story of unpaid toil. One case was more than five years old. Hai, a 45-year-old man who had worked continuously for ten years in the construction industry, showed us a piece of worn paper on which was written, "XXX owes Hai three thousand yuan only." The debtor's signature made this piece of paper the only evidence of a debt owed to the worker.

Every time we ran into cases of debt, we enquired into the debt and the reasons for non-payment. A typical story was:

> "This debt paper is just waste paper. It's useless now to ask for money. The subcontractor claimed he had no money. He was a shark," a worker said. "Do you mean that the subcontractor intentionally kept your money or that he couldn't pay you because the money didn't come through?" we asked. "Who knows? We didn't know who the boss was. We haven't even seen the boss."

The boss the workers mentioned was not the labor-supplier subcontractor but the second- or third-level contractor who outsourced the work. The subcontractor, however, was the only one responsible for wage payment, because he recruited the workers, even though he was not the boss in a legal sense.[17]

In this village, most of the labor-supplier subcontractors recruited from their own or surrounding villages. After the Chinese New Year holiday, subcontractors used their networks in the village to recruit a group of workers, the exact number depending on the size of the construction project, and promised a daily rate for both skilled workers and unskilled workers. All the workers knew that their wages would be paid after the completion of the project or at the end of the year; this practice had already become common among the workers in the village. As long as they could be sure to receive their wages by the time they returned home to help with the harvest or to celebrate Chinese New Year, they consented to the delayed payment, though not altogether willingly. In the village, non-industrial social relationships are manipulated to serve the purpose of labor expropriation and to disguise the relationship between wage-labor and capital. As a consequence, the "real" boss has become something of a myth in the construction industry.

The construction workers' hope that they will be paid eventually relies on kin connections and villager networks. A saying popular among the workers, especially from the older generation, is: "A monk may run away but a temple stays," implying that the subcontractor also has relatives in the village and it would be difficult to avoid his responsibilities. However, this belief became increasingly shaky when wage arrears and debts became routine in the late 1990s. The non-commodified social relationships were gradually destroyed through the labor subcontracting system. When the problem of wage arrears became serious, conflicts between subcontractors and villagers occurred more frequently and their relationship worsened.

A number of workers emphasized that every year they looked for a new small subcontractor, always hoping he would be better than the previous one but, when jobs were badly needed, the workers, especially middle-aged ones, had little choice. Even if the subcontractor had a poor record in wage payments, there was still hope that he would be able to pay at the end of the Lunar Year.

By the time we visited the village in Hebei, there were serious worries among the workers that the subcontractors would run off without paying the wages owed. Many villagers complained that, as more people were hired as construction workers, the social relationships within the rural community became more tense. Complaints often came from both sides of the employer/employee divide. One subcontractor, for example, complained that one of his workers had just left the construction team without saying a word: "This is not a normal industry. You don't have a long-term relationship with anybody. People just leave the construction site whenever they like." The complaints of subcontractors about their workers were as frequent as the complaints that workers made about their subcontractors. Trust was very much in decline, seriously damaging the entire social fabric of the village.

CONCLUSION

The lives of construction workers are seldom recorded or studied, as if they are not significant. The postmodern play of "immaterial" labor further marginalized their voices and existence. In fact, as pioneers of "materialized" labor, Chinese construction workers were highly praised and lauded for their labor in the socialist period. This symbolic effect was abruptly shifted in reform-era China when labor was turned into a commodity and attributed a market value. With skewed class forces in opposition to capital, Chinese construction workers were poorly situated in a specific political economy where there is no boss, no employer directly responsible for employment practices in the industry. The capital–labor relationship has been entirely disguised: workers literally do not know the identity of the developers and the construction companies who are ultimately responsible for the non-payment of the wages owed to them. This mis-recognition has been made possible through the labor subcontracting system; an invisible hand, the market, operating several steps removed from the workforce, enables a rigged losing hand to be dealt out to a transient army of labor.

The exceptional practices involved in the rapidly changing construction industry induce angry, largely radical collective actions by construction workers. The political economy of the industry shapes a specific labor subcontracting system that embodies two processes: the rapid commodification of labor in the rural villages and the expropriation of labor in the production process of the construction sector in the urban areas. Rural non-industrial social relationships have been manipulated to serve the process of labor expropriation, which in turn has destroyed social trust and intensified the labor conflicts at the construction site.

Today, construction workers are the "invisible" subjects of the city that they have built. They were present when what is now prime land in the city was still wasteland, having no economic value to society. They disappear once the buildings have been constructed with their toil, and the value of the land has escalated. The workers are absent in the space that they have created and too frequently are not paid the wages that they have worked for. In short, the labor subcontracting system is a core problem of the construction industry, generating a culture of violence that gets acted out in both destructive and self-destructive forms.

4 | Making and Unmaking of the New Chinese Working Class

A paradox was created when *Time* magazine elected workers in China as among the runners-up for the 2009 Person of the Year by commenting that Chinese workers had brightened the future of humanity by "leading the world to economic recovery."[1] In 2010, 18 young migrant workers attempted suicide at Foxconn production facilities in China, bringing Foxconn to the attention of global consumers. More than 1.4 million workers, who had been placed in the "best" Foxconn factory-cum-dormitory, seemed only to experience more anxiety and see fewer alternatives than their peers. The new generation of Chinese workers perceived themselves as losing their futures, but preparing for their own battles, a necessary historical process for instigating its own class.

A specter is haunting China – not global capital, but a new working class embodied with great forces of suppression and of resistance. Today, many people still refuse to acknowledge the existence of the new laboring subject as a class force as it reflects only a ghostly shadow. The calling of the new working class becomes more anxious and compelling when Foxconn workers keep on jumping to their deaths.[2] The specter of the new working class now looks for its own fresh blood. Its incarnation lies in the fact that China has turned into the "factory of the world," placing itself squarely at the core of global capitalism over the past three decades. No one will deny this fact – the rise of China. China is admired by its international competitors because of its supreme capability in producing not only low-end goods but also high-value and high-tech products. Then the question remains: why do

Chinese workers who are producing state-of-the-art consumer products such as iPhones and iPads try to kill themselves? While China rises, are Chinese workers losing it?[3]

A FAREWELL TO CLASS

The politics of the making and remaking of the Chinese working class has been greatly changed when compared to the discussion in *Made in China: The Women Factory Workers in a Global Workplace* (Pun 2005). The screams and dreams that threaded the lives of the first generation of women workers have now given way to deaths and protests that are the lived experiences of the second generation of peasant-workers of both sexes. At the turn of the new century, the rapid making of the new working class seems just like the sun struggling to come out in the very early morning. It has been present at its own making. China's "world factory" inevitably constitutes and is constituted by this newly emerged working class. It is high time we make some sense of it.

The struggle to be a part of this new working class, however, is replete with blood, sweat, and tears. Notwithstanding the predominant structural factor that has shaped the Chinese working class, the "delinking" between class structure and class identity, between class consciousness and class action still largely exist. The reform hegemony, the neoliberal policies, and the western discourse on class all contribute to this "delinking" of class. The reform hegemony coincided with a western "farewell to class" discourse that firmly rejects the existence of the class issue in post-socialist China. Just like the argument on "the end of history" that contributed to the birth of neoliberalism in post-socialist countries, a discourse on "farewell to class" directly led to the death of "class analysis" in China. Nowhere could we see a displacement of class conflicts from the West to the East so successfully achieved and have this displacement subsumed as a "postmodern play" of class language.

A Western society without a critical mass of industrial workers seems to mean a society without class and labor! The trends of post-structuralism and postmodernism further shifted the focus from the sphere of relations of production to the sphere of civil society and consumption, at best, a study of middle class and consumption. It is an obvious misunderstanding that post-structuralist studies could not enhance our understanding of class and labor, especially regarding the issues of agency and subjectivity. The death of "class analysis" was, however, a prevalent statement everywhere in the West (Lichtenstein 2006). Fewer and fewer studies on class and labor were published. Departments of history, sociology, and political science once considered class to be the crucial area of focus; by the beginning of the twenty-first century, hardly any courses on class or labor studies could be found in their curricula. Influenced by Western hegemony, mainstream Chinese scholars instead were happy to follow suit and sought shelter in the declaration of the death of class analysis in the West to affirm the neoliberal project of Chinese reformist transformation.

The "death" of class in the West is hence reflected and imagined in its second death in China, resisting fiercely to recognize that its death represents an incarnation of the new working class in the Third World. Placing China squarely at the heart of global capital accumulation and the new international division of labor, we see not only offshore capital flight, but also that class conflicts have been rapidly exported to developing countries. We call for a return of class from a Third World perspective to look at the change in Chinese society in the reform era.

I attempt to pose a paradox: at a time when China is turning itself into the "factory of the world," the political hegemony, both in the West and in China, is seeking to emulate the process of class subsumption at the expense of the rise of the new working class, and the new laboring subjects have emerged alongside global production. There is a hegemonic project undertaken by a "quest for globality," driven by neoliberal political ideologies in unmaking this new class force. This paradoxical process is nevertheless embodied in a complex historicity of "class and revolution," a specific Maoist practice of class struggle in China's socialist period. The abrupt denunciation of Mao's class struggle paved the way for the twisted subsumption of class discourse in the globalizing reform period.

THE HOLLOWING OUT OF "CLASS"

If it is the death, and not life, of migrant workers that speaks out against the fact that Chinese workers will be the beneficiaries of the new global economy in its international division of labor, and that compels us to make sense of the formation of a new class and of its struggles in contemporary China, we immediately face an irony: the language of "class" has been paradoxically emptied out. We were perplexed to understand a strange but cruel life experience: the lived experience of class is very acute for Chinese workers; however, the discourse of class is seriously subdued in public life. The discourse of class has not only been displaced by the hegemonic project of neoliberal China, but it is also widely abhorred by the common people, not only the newly emerged urban middle class, but sometimes the working class itself. The self-denunciation of class subjects themselves further suffocates a class discourse, which could work to articulate class identity and collectivity.

We see that this discursive dyslexia concerning class has a tremendous effect on policy and institutional controls on population and labor issues in China, and it not only constrains labor mobility, work opportunities, and settlement communities, but also the formation of the working class itself. The "unfinished" class composed of the new worker-subjects who have been officially and politically identified as peasant-workers, *mingong*, represents a process of proletarianization that is not yet complete in today's China. We see a new Chinese working class struggling to be born at the very moment when the language of "class" has been silenced. The formation of a new working class in contemporary China has been checked structurally by these discursive and institutional effects.

The process of "proletarianization" in socialist China was unique in that political forces rather than market forces dictated the whole process. In the first place, Maoism provided a reinterpretation of Marx's class analysis in Chinese society by highlighting class struggles in rural societies as well as in urban cities. As early as 1926, Mao Zedong in his famous article, "Analysis of the classes in Chinese society", argued that the reason for offering an analysis of classes in Chinese society was to identify enemies and friends for the Communist Revolution: "Who are our enemies? Who are our friends? This is a question of the first importance for the revolution" (1965 [1926]: 13). Mao stated that "the leading force in our revolution is the industrial proletariat." However, in early twentieth-century China, the modern industrial proletariat only numbered about two million, and "these two million industrial workers are mainly employed in five industries – railways, mining, maritime transport, textiles and ship-building – and a great number are enslaved in enterprises owned by foreign capitalists" (Mao 1965 [1926]: 18–19). Mao understood that the number of industrial proletariat was still small in prewar China, even though he had high expectations about the participation of this class in the revolution. The subsequent revolution and the wars against Japan and the Guomindang actually relied on the vast peasantry in the rural areas, who, nevertheless, were classified by Mao as semi-proletariat and the surest allies of the proletariat.[4]

However, after the liberation, it was the urban subjects, not the rural masses, who were proclaimed as the avant-garde of the Chinese proletariat, and thus they were the owners of the new China. One of the revolutionary goals of this new Chinese proletariat was to keep class struggles alive in order to safeguard the socialist revolution. The

Chinese working class in the Maoist period, unlike its embryonic form in the 1920s, was formed within a short period – a few years under a command economy, in contrast to the English or other European working classes, whose formation, dictated by the market economy, took at least half a century. State-owned and collective enterprises were built rapidly with an emphasis on the construction of heavy industry in order to safeguard China from the West. Not only were jobs allocated to urban workers who held urban *hukou,* state-owned and collective enterprises were formulated as "units," which served as encompassing social institutions to guarantee the new working class employment, housing, education, and medical care. The role of the party-state was required to intervene in production, reproduction, and consumption, and hence when the planned economy was accomplished, the process of "socialist proletarianization" was also complete in Maoist China. In this process, Chinese worker-subjects were interpellated with a "class identity" or "status" by the Maoist concept of class.

This political articulation of Mao's class concept unfortunately led to an essentialized discourse of class identity, which at times proved incapable of stimulating political transformation from below (Wang 2013). Thus after the Chinese Liberation in 1949, the whole population was interpellated with a class identity/status according to a classification from pre-liberation "class" backgrounds: landlords, rich peasants, middle peasants, poor peasants, and farm laborers in the rural areas; and revolutionary cadre, revolutionary military men, professionals, workers, store sales, bourgeoisie, industrial and commercial capitalists, small merchants, handicraft workers, poor people, vagabonds, and so on in urban areas. After the socialist reform in 1955 and 1956, these class categories were radically simplified into two major class identities in the city: cadres and workers. Until the end of the Cultural Revolution, the frequent official classification was into two classes (working class and peasantry class) plus one additional stratum (the intellectuals).

In reformed China, the textuality of class was rapidly shattered when Deng Xiaoping launched the reform and open-door policies at the beginning of the 1980s. After the June Fourth Movement, especially after the Southern Tour of Deng Xiaoping to Shenzhen in 1992, to reaffirm his reform policies, Deng openly proclaimed that the party-state had to guard against radicalism from the left more than from the right. The Chinese working class, previously provided with a structural context by state enterprises or collective enterprises – with a job and a class position – was forced to go (Walder 1991; Sargeson 1999). Together with state bureaucrats, the newly emerged bourgeoisie and urban middle class looked to a neoliberal discourse of modernity to create a "step down" for this working class, which was once the protagonist of the socialist country. The Maoist language of "class struggle" was permanently abandoned, and the privileged position of the Chinese working class denounced. The paradox of class history in China is that at this particular moment of denunciation, a new laboring subject was quickly formed by rural migrant workers who poured into the newly industrialized or development zones, which constituted the base for global capital-seeking by tapping into the huge quantities of labor in China. Thus, a new working class comprising vast numbers of peasant-workers from rural China was striving to be born. Later they were joined by the laid-off workers from state enterprises and collectives who were forced to seek their survival in the market. This newly formed Chinese working class, however, was obstructed at the very moment of its birth as a class force. When the class-in-itself was structurally germinating, the hegemonic blocs had no mercy for this working class, and attempted to contain it by various techniques of power. The class struggle lies again in the creation of a "class-for-itself."

If we say that it was Mao's revolutionary ideas that engendered the "class struggle" – and hence class in China – then it was Deng's reforms that announced the death of "class" by replacing a "modernity" discourse with a promise to allow "a proportion of people to get rich first" – the stratum that was ambitious and capable of climbing up. "Speaking trauma" in the early 1980s, initially as an intellectual project from the victimized "rightists" to disclose the "evils of the Cultural Revolution," helped denounce Mao and his belief in "class struggle" in making history. A farewell to "Mao," and thus a farewell to "Marx," rapidly became the common motto for the political ideology of power and the new elite. There is no doubt that the post-socialist party machine turned its hegemony upside down by targeting the "class" language when society itself was undergoing a rapid process of capitalization, and when class was going through a rapid process of making and remaking.

THE RETURN TO CLASS AND THE NEW GENERATION OF WORKERS

However, it is against this paradoxical historical moment that the specters of Marx are returning. A new Chinese working class is struggling to be born. The formation of the new Chinese worker-subjects, *dagongmei* or *dagongza*, with all their struggles, richness, heterogeneity and multiple working locations, can no longer be described or politicized as an abstract class subject, as the worker-subjects experience, make sense, react, and project their life trajectories in contemporary China. As a weapon of social struggle, class analysis, if useful, can only be reactivated by rooting it in class experience from below, that is, for instance, in the everyday micro-politics of a labor regime in which the Chinese workers themselves are in confrontation with capital and the market. The new laboring subjects have to live out their own class experience as part of their life struggles in concrete lived spaces. And if the worker-subject was once traumatically interpellated by a language of class from above, then the new subjects that have emerged at the intersection of global capitalism and the Chinese modernity project invoke a desire for a return to "class analysis" on the production lines, in the workshops, at the workers' dormitories, a space where the workers live out their own complexities and their conflictual life experiences. If "class analysis" is already a dead language in today's China, the re-articulation of the new "*dagong*" subjectivity in post-socialist China is, nevertheless, a timely project.

If it was once said the previous generation of women factory workers was subjected to suffering, anxiety, and bodily pain, and like Yan, a typical woman, was compelled to scream, expropriating her own body as a weapon against a time of China's becoming a factory to the world in the early 1990s (Pun 2005), the new generation of peasant-workers has now made up their mind to take action and launch collective struggles in the 2000s. We take gender and class as seriously involving both sexes and probe deeply into looking at how the hierarchy and power created in the workplace affected the collective actions in the interplay between class and gender in terms of leadership, mobilization, and participation.

In fact, peasant-workers (*nongmin gong*) are not a new phenomenon in China. They were well represented in prewar China, and they were frequently employed as temporary labor in state or collective enterprises in the socialist period (Perry 1993; Walder 1986). When we refer to the first generation of migrant workers, we mean those born in the late 1960s and the 1970s who were the first to move from the countryside to work in the newly industrialized zones of South China in the 1980s and 1990s. The pioneers were the female workers who came to work in the toy and electronics factories in Shekou Industrial Zone of Shenzhen where China's first SEZ was formulated (Lee 1998; Pun 2005). The second generation of peasant-workers refers to those who were born or raised during the reform period (i.e., those born in the late 1970s and 1980s, who entered the working world in the late 1990s and 2000s). There was no break between the first and second generation of migrant workers, only the accumulation of work experiences leading to a change in the workers' perception of capital and the state, and a shared understanding of themselves as peasant-worker, a specific class position in today's China.

Notwithstanding all the difficulties, we could draw a timeline to distinguish the first and second generation of Chinese workers, along which we could observe new life expectations and dispositions, nuanced meanings of work, and more collective labor actions for those who have grown up during the reform period and entered the labor market in the early 2000s. The way of life for the second generation was characterized by more individualistic dispositions, increased proclivity to urban consumer culture, less economic burden, and more personal pursuit of development and freedom, and yet higher job turnover and less loyalty to their work, and simultaneously more spontaneous collective actions in the workplace. The second generation, born and raised in the reform period, was relatively better educated, materially well-off but spiritually disoriented, while having a cosmopolitan outlook. The rapid economic growth in the reform era shaped a social structure in which the second generation experienced a deeper rural–urban chasm, greater income inequality, and increased social exclusion, despite constant improvement in their working and living conditions. The huge divide between their expectations of becoming urban worker-citizens and their actual daily work experiences, contained in the dormitory labor regime, excluding them from city life, precipitated anger, frustration, and resentment conducive to the emergence of the workers' consciousness and their shared class position.

THE UNFINISHED PROLETARIANIZATION

You Need To Stand Up
You say your life is destined to a state of wandering
You did and you picked up this passage
Never gonna regret
Even though you have to suffer tremendous difficulties
You chose this route to becoming nobody

Care about you, your friends
You can't say that you have no way of return
Everybody has his time of hardship and haplessness
Undergoing all these sufferings
No matter how
You need to stand up, you need to stand up

A poem in a workers' newsletter

QUASI IDENTITY AS PEASANT-WORKERS

We set out to make sense of the increasingly complex struggle of the new Chinese working class, now in its second generation. E. P. Thompson, in his classic work *The Making of the English Working Class*, put it clearly: class formation is "an active process," which owes as much to agency as to conditioning, and which embodies a notion of historical relationship (1966: 9).

Considering the world history of labor, the formation and maturity of the working class usually took root in its second and third generation of rural workers who came to work in industrial cities. The suffering, hardships, and grievances of working lives often reached their peak not in the first generation of workers but in the subsequent ones. This is the process of proletarianization, which turns agricultural laborers into industrial workers, either voluntarily or involuntarily, that runs through the history of world capitalism.[5]

When China transformed itself into the world's factory and became a contemporary industrialized society, it re-enacted a common phenomenon in the global history of capitalism.[6] What is special about China is its peculiar process of proletarianization: in order to incorporate the Chinese socialist system into the global economy, rural workers are called upon to work in the city but not to stay in the city. For China's new working class, industrialization and urbanization are still two highly disconnected processes as the peasant-workers were deprived of their right to live where they work.[7] In brief, the process of proletarianization of Chinese peasant-workers was shaped by a spatial separation of production in urban areas and reproduction in the countryside. This separation of spheres, however, was overturned by the rise of a dormitory labor regime, which offered a new combination of work and "home," and resembled early capitalist work and residence arrangements (Pun and Smith 2007).

Among 270 million migrant laborers, more than 150 million who have been drawn from rural China to work in coastal industrial areas and who, for three decades, have toiled in foreign or privately owned factories, are still deprived of the legal and social right to reside in the city or to set up their own working-class community. This segregation is driven by political and economic factors and further supported by legal and administrative measures, especially manipulating the *hukou* system that preserves and prolongs the rural–urban divide. Migrant workers are uprooted, but this experience has never stopped them from ceaselessly trying to stay in the city, either as temporary sojourners or *de facto* urban residents, jumping from workplace to workplace, and city to city. The second generation of migrant workers has realized that they will always be considered second-class citizens by urban governments, which recognize no obligation to provide them with housing, medical care, education, or other social services.

The resulting pattern is an unfinished process of proletarianization, which leads to a deepening sense of becoming incomplete, that is, of becoming a peasant-worker (a "quasi" or "half" worker in the industrial world). The individual, suffering from a sense of inadequacy, is subjected to a process of wandering. Almost all the workers we studied in the industrial districts of Shenzhen and Dongguan in the past decade, most of them aged between 16 and 32, had experienced changing their job once a year or after less than a year. Most of them had already worked in the city for a number of years and only a very small proportion of them would consider that they had a good chance of staying in the city. The urban and industrial world still did not belong to the second generation of migrant workers. The peasant-worker has nowhere to go and nowhere to stay, as shown in the worker's poem: "You say your life is destined to a state of wandering" and "you chose this route to becoming nobody" because you are neither a *nongmin* (peasant) nor a *gongren* (worker). You are always a *nongmin gong* (peasant-worker), somebody caught in between a rural citizen and a worker – a social identity which is always quasi. Acquiring this quasi-identity, the individual, however, feels responsible for himself or herself and is compelled to try to overcome the difficulties of becoming: "Never gonna regret, even though you have to suffer tremendous difficulties." This is the motto of the new generation of *dagong* workers, who are trying to overcome their experience of incompleteness.[8]

XIN'S STORY: THE HIDDEN INJURY OF CLASS

I knew Xin, a migrant factory worker in Shenzhen, for a number of years before the research team and I followed him for his year-long labor rights action and with a visit to his home village in Henan in May 2008. We highlight Xin, a male worker aged 32, because we take him to be representative of the new generation of peasant-workers, whose silence has become anger, whose pain has become action, and whose consent has become refusal (Pun and Lu 2010b). We entered Xin's life during his prolonged pursuit of workers' interests and rights by means of a series of collective actions which will be discussed in the final chapter. By the time we met Xin, he and his four co-workers had already left their place of work – a factory in Shenzhen that supplied Disney toys. In February 2007 when Xin left, he was a skilled worker and foreman of a department specializing in crafting molds. He had been working in the city since 1998, a year after his unsuccessful attempt to enter university. Over the course of ten years, Xin rose from an ordinary worker to a skilled craftsman to a foreman responsible for a team of skilled workers. He had worked for three companies. We were aware of his pride in himself at working so diligently and intelligently that he proved himself a good worker-subject, worthy to have a position of responsibility in a modern factory producing world-famous Disney toys.

Xin quit his job at the Disney supplier factory after working there for one year so that he could take part in a collective action against the company. He recalled that, when he left the factory gates, he found himself with no way forward and no way back. He was lost in the city where he had been working for ten years and where he had met with some success in his career: "Never gonna regret...undergoing all these sufferings, no matter how, you need to stand up, you need to stand up."

Unlike Yan, a pioneer of the first generation of peasant-workers who was lost and became inarticulate when she left her factory in Dongguan in the mid-1990s,[9] Xin now found himself not only with a sense of loss, but he also experienced an overwhelming anger the moment he stepped out of the factory's dormitory compound. He decided "to do something big": he was not at all "calm and balanced," even though he was ambivalent about his loss and anger.

The plight of the peasant-worker is so well established that even the workers we met in Shenzhen and Dongguan who had been employed in the cities for more than ten years still found it impossible to reside there. The longer they work in a big city, the more aware they are of their exclusion. Rural migrant workers could sometimes stay in the city after a few years of working in a factory if they could become small storeowners, hawkers, or garbage collectors. However, they remain displaced and transient residents, with no hope of becoming proper citizens. This is a defining feature of the proletarianization of the first and second generations of migrant workers.

THE REFORM: FREEDOM AND "HOMING"

Xin, who was born in 1977, grew up in the years of the reform. He was among the 120 million rural migrant workers who went to the city and part of the second generation of *dagong* workers. If we argue that the reform was the catalyst for this unfinished proletarianization, then the new rural–urban divide provides the social conditions that have withstood the great influx of rural to urban migration. China is still experiencing increasing inequality in its rural–urban income distribution. As the reform continues, the widening gap between rural and urban lives is not only reflected in living standards but also in the mode of life itself. The social chasm is further widened. For the second generation of the new working class, the urge to move out of the village and transform themselves is even stronger than it was for the first generation.

Now the emptying of rural communities is no longer a matter of concern but a matter of fact in many parts of China (Yan 2008). The feeling of inadequacy or not being able to catch up with the migration wave is a symbol of incompleteness of the self for young people in villages. Xin looked back at his life and recalled the three times that he failed the entrance exams for university. After failing again in 1998, he gave up completely, even though his father opposed his decision: "I know people who tried seven or eight times without success, and then collapsed. I needed to put a stop to it before it was too late. Maybe I would make my way elsewhere." He was also ashamed of his dependency on his young sister for economic support. She went to work in Shenzhen immediately after finishing junior middle school in 1994.[10]

As Xin observed, "My younger sister who graduated from the junior middle school has moved to work in the city for a number of years, yet I am still staying in the village repeating my exams." Going to *dagong* not only means the ability to earn money to support one's family but also fosters a sense of individual independence and freedom. Not being able to work like his younger sister was a source of pain for Xin. Seeking freedom by moving to *dagong* is the common desire of rural workers, a desire that has deepened through the generations. Katznelson and Zolberg (1986) have argued that disposition and habitus are the most significant ingredients in the formation of a working class.

We maintain that the first moment for the new Chinese working class to identify itself and the main disposition that characterizes the Chinese working class is the shared desire to move out to *dagong*. In China, the process of proletarianization is largely self-driven, arising from the strong sense of acquiring freedom to *dagong* within a context of the huge rural–urban divide in the age of rapid industrialization and globalization of the reform period.

For the first generation of migrant workers, moving to *dagong* was not only a major trend (when a person successfully moved out to *dagong*, the whole village would follow) but also a means of realizing economic goals. These goals included building a new house, financing a sibling's education, marrying, and setting up a small business. Although in the 1980s and 1990s they were often depicted by the media as visionless migrants traveling without a clear direction, they did have specific goals (Zhang 2001). Today, the new generation of migrant workers is less motivated by economic goals and more determined to achieve personal development, freedom, and a different way of life. The yearning for *dagong* is stronger than ever. In Xin's village in Henan, home to about 200 families, almost all the inhabitants of working age have departed. More than ten entire families have moved out of the village. The study of Xin's village echoes the findings of various researchers on rural communities in Central China (Fang 2003; Yan 2008). Fang's (2003) study in Hubei shows that in a village with a population of 352 individuals of working age (15–59), 148 of them moved out to *dagong* for the whole year, leaving only 204 in the village. As a result of the reform, the urban world seems open to them, even though they soon realize that this openness is severely limited.

In 1998, Xin finally set out to work in a small factory in Shenzhen. The working conditions were as appalling as in other factories in the same industrial village. During his probation period, he was paid only seven yuan a day. Once he passed his probation, his wages could be raised to eight yuan a day. At the small factory, which produced converters for TV antennas, he worked from 7 a.m. to 12 p.m. and from 12:30 p.m. to 11:00 p.m. Even more dehumanizing was the treatment workers received from the factory supervisor. On one occasion, the supervisor asked Xin to remove a lead-bonder from the floor. The lead-bonder had just finished melting and was still extremely hot. Xin, a new worker, was not aware of the danger and picked it up without gloves. All his fingers were badly burned. He remembers, "The supervisor stood by my side. He was laughing, looking at how a live person got hurt but not treating my wounds. After having a good laugh, he ordered me to do other work." After only seven days of employment, Xin was dismissed.

The reform gave this generation the freedom to move, which led to the freedom to work for foreign or privately owned enterprises and the freedom to leave their home town. It unleashed their desire to transform themselves but, in doing so, they were forced to undergo the process of selling their labor to the factory owners, the new owners of today's China. This is no secret. The dialectic of the reform lies in the very process of freeing rural subjects so that they can transform themselves into laboring bodies, while at the same time it severely limits their freedom in the industrial city. Xin was free to move and to work. But once he acted freely, he found that he had lost the freedom to progress or retreat. He was now a stranger and a permanent transient in the city. He soon lost his sense of "home" and felt like a man with no place to go.

Xin continued his account of his first factory job:

On the seventh day, a few co-workers who came from my hometown could tolerate it no more. They were ready to quit. One of them asked me to go too. But I said no. I wanted to continue to work till I received my wages. We kept talking for about ten minutes at the entrance of the shop floor. Our boss noticed us and turned to a supervisor. When I returned to the shop floor, the supervisor did not ask me anything. He just said, "You need not come tomorrow." I then told my co-villager who had arranged the job for me that I was fired. I should have been given 49 yuan for my seven days of work. My co-villager said, "You dare to ask for money! You should be pleased that you haven't been fined!"

Xin had worked for seven days but had earned nothing. He took his personal belongings and left the factory:

> In those days, I didn't have a temporary residential permit. I was wandering on the streets, afraid to walk on the main roads or to enter small alleys, where I feared I would be robbed. At night, I had nowhere to go except cinemas…After 11 p.m., the cinema played late shows at 3 yuan a ticket. The 100-person cinema house was then transformed into a place to sleep for as many as 40 to 50 people. I couldn't even straighten my legs. Between 6 and 7 a.m., we were asked to go. I slept in the cinema for more than 20 nights until I found another job.

Xin's story echoes the majority of the migrant workers who had similar experiences in their first move to the city for *dagong*. Ming, a female worker in an electronics factory in Shenzhen, said, "The first thing I learned from my first job is that you don't have your own right. The boss has the right to ask you to leave but you don't have it."

The reform embodies a contradiction: as new labor was needed for the use of capital, Chinese peasants were asked to transform themselves into laboring bodies, willing to spend their days in the workplace. This represented a departure from time-honored customs, rituals, traditions, and cultures – their entire previous ways of living and their history. Yet as disposable labor, when they were not needed, they were asked to go back to the villages that they had been induced to forsake and to which they had failed to remain loyal, particularly for the younger generation. If transience was a dominant characteristic of the first generation of migrant workers (Pun 2005: 5), rupture characterizes the second generation, who now spend much more of their lives in urban areas. Transience suggests transitions, and so encourages hopes and dreams of transformation. Rupture, however, creates closure: there is no hope of either transforming oneself into an urban worker or of returning to the rural community to take up life as a peasant.

NO RETURN: NEW FORMS OF ENCLOSURE

Dance, dance, dance, someone says what I dance is a dance of survival
Dance, dance, dance, what we dance is pain and anger
Who take away our humanity and dignity
Together with skinny shoulders
Creeping on the alien land haplessly
"Rewriting Grasshopper," written by a young worker in 2006

In the spring of 2000, after working two years in the city, Xin made up his mind to go back to his home town. Xin told us: "Even though I worked hard every day, I was not treated as a human being in the workplace. I didn't see I would have a future in the city. How could I have a prospect? I had no money or anything to rely on. I would rather go back home." Having no place in the city, Xin found no future or prospect for prolonging his working life in the urban areas. In contrast to many workers of his generation who still maintained themselves in the city, Xin was determined to return to the place where he had been born and nurtured. He still had a hope of doing business in rural areas even though he was not really committed to rural development in general or recognized himself as a rural subject in particular.

The struggle between going out to *dagong* or staying in the rural village hoping for some development was the preoccupation of two generations of the working class. A study in 2007 on the business conditions of returned migrants conducted by the Development

Research Center of the State Council further states that among 301 villages from 28 provinces, returned migrants accounted for 23 percent of the total existing migrant laborers, and among those who returned, 16.06 percent had participated in setting up rural enterprises or doing agricultural business (Han and Cui 2007). Our own studies on existing migrant laborers in Shenzhen and Dongguan, however, show that, among 1,455 workers, less than 20 percent had planned to return home to work (see Han and Cui 2007).

It has often been presumed that the rural areas would be the final resort for migrant workers who had lost their job in the city. Sustained by the existing land use system, the village would bear the social costs of reproduction of its laborers. This argument was often supported by the fact that, once workers left their factories, they would temporarily return to their home towns for a few weeks. The strong desire to return, particularly for the Chinese New Year, was demonstrated in 2008 when, despite incessant snowstorms causing hundreds of deaths and thousands of injuries, a great wave of laborers came home. In many workers' diaries and journals, the phrases "missing home" and "dreaming of going home" recur. Such nostalgia could be understood as the "weapon of the weak" in the face of the cruelty of industrial life. "Home" becomes their imaginary anchor to life.

However, the second generation of peasant-workers was soon to discover that their lived experience was a radical disavowal of this assumption, which had sustained the previous generation. In contrast to the formation of the English working class in the late eighteenth and nineteenth centuries, the new Chinese working class had not undergone the brutal process of a land enclosure movement, nor was it forced by the state to give up their land tenure. Instead, the land rights of the agrarian population based on male lines of succession were protected, even though there have been heated debates about the privatization of rural land and obvious erosions of peasants' land rights in the last decade (Qin 2006). Chinese peasants were still able to keep for themselves a small piece of land sufficient to sustain a life of basic subsistence. The final cancellation of the agriculture tax in 2006 further eased the burdens of peasant life. Unlike the English working class, there was indeed no coercion to enforce a process of proletarianization. However, the fact that there are no compulsory measures to force peasants to leave their land has not made a difference. For the second generation of the working class, due to the worsening situation in the life of peasants and the loss of the means of subsistence, which depends on the soil, the sense of "enclosure" was acute. Xin remembered his return to his hometown:

> When I got back home (in March 2000), it was the time of seeding for the coming year. I was thrilled because I had a great plan in my mind. I subcontracted a piece of waste land to set up an agricultural business. I couldn't sleep at night, because I was obsessed with the idea that if I could expand the scale of the cash-crop plantation, I could also make money. I could show to my parents and the villagers that returning home was a good move.

Xin began by mobilizing his relatives and neighbors: "I could do it because I made a tremendous effort to convince people and I had a good network in the village." Xin was pleased. Others provided tractors and farm labor. He was able to acquire around 20 mu of arable land to start his plan. After conducting a local market survey, Xin decided to grow watermelons, a fruit he thought would be easy to manage and have market potential. However, circumstances were against him, as they usually are in rural lives. Due to heavy rains, the watermelons ripened too soon to be sold. From the outset, Xin's father, who was experienced in farming and who knew the risks of agricultural production and the fluctuations of the market, had objected to the subcontracting project. Behind Xin's back, his father urged the others to withdraw their support. After just a few months, almost all Xin's savings of several thousand yuan had gone. He had no choice: he had to leave his hometown to find work again.

Acting like a capitalist set upon an enclosure to the life of peasants, the opposition of Xin's father to Xin's plan also reached a degree of enclosure: there was no way he would let his son stay in the country because there is no future there in his eyes. Xin's strong "will to return" encountered his father's strong "will of refusal," revealing the life struggles between the father and the son. The victory of his father's refusal undermined Xin's strong desire to return, resulting in a similar sense of enclosure, both spiritual and physical.

Xin was definitely not alone in this "enclosure" experience. For those who decided to return home to do business either in small towns or villages, less than half went back to the village. And of those who actually returned to the village and invested in agricultural businesses, most we met in Shenzhen and Dongguan ended up losing money. Hua, a female worker who returned home to get married and to work in agriculture in a village in West Guangdong, said, "I lost five thousand in three months' time for raising ducks in my home town. I don't have experience in feeding ducks. Many ducks died and I lost money. That is why you see me again." When they reached the age to marry, usually between 22 and 26, female workers would return home, get married, and move in with their husband's family, and some of them would end up doing small business in the town. Hua, however, came back to Shenzhen for *dagong* after only a half-year break in the village. No experience and skill working in an agricultural business, lacking resources and finance to set up a business, and a highly fluctuating market all contributed to negative outcomes for the businesses of returned migrant workers, despite the recent government policy of encouraging return migration for the construction of new rural villages.

The visit to Xin's village in Henan also revealed the same situation. Only a few households were involved in doing agricultural business and one of the them was Xin's uncle who had subcontracted a fish pond, a lotus root plantation pond, and raised a few heads of pig and sheep. Despite the fact that the family worked very hard to take care of their business, Xin's uncle and aunt both said they could hardly earn 10,000 yuan a year even though they had contributed three laborers to the business. Had Xin stayed on and kept running his business, he might have had difficulty in surpassing the achievements of his uncle.

Xin had no choice but to leave his hometown again. This time he was traumatized. Internalizing his pain, he traveled to Shenzhen. On the train to Shenzhen, he overheard someone say that good money could be made by doing sculptures. He was hired at a handicraft factory where he earned 800 yuan a month. After a probation period, his wages increased steadily. In his third year at the factory (2002), he earned up to 1,700 yuan per month. With overtime, he sometimes earned 3,000 yuan a month.

Xin was lucky enough to rise to the position of master craftsman and earn a high salary. However, because of the trauma he had suffered, Xin never really felt happy in his working life. If the pursuit of material rewards is the shared ambition overriding internal differences among the working class, the pursuit had lost its meaning for Xin. The concept of working life was blighted for him, creating a rupture in his life: "Wherever I work, I don't feel happy. My heart doesn't rest in calmness. I always feel that I should do some big thing."

The second generation of migrant workers was left with limited choice: "I missed my home while I was out to *dagong*. When I returned home, I thought of going out again." Only a small percentage of the migrant workers are willing to return home for individual development and yet, like Xin, they find no way to return. The majority of the second generation nevertheless had realized that the existing rural community means "no development" and hence "no return." "Farming has no value" becomes common sense to the peasant-workers. In fact, they know that the new house they built, together with marriage expenses, education fees, medical treatment costs, and all household facilities they could buy, etc., were the product of the earnings they had from *dagong*. The social reproduction of labor in terms of housing, clothing, education, and medical care except food relied almost entirely on the incomes they earned from *dagong*. It is debatable whether it is still possible to argue that the cost of social reproduction is borne by the rural communities. The lack of room for individual development for returning migrants and the inability to take up the social costs of reproduction in the rural communities further create a sense of "enclosure" of land, resulting in what we understood as a process of "self-driven" proletarianization.

The emptying out of the rural communities was imbued with material conditions as well as a spiritual sense. For the younger generation, who have grown up in relatively good living conditions, who have a more cosmopolitan outlook, and who care about what color to dye their hair and what style of clothing to wear, now it is even harder to have a way to return once they embark on their *dagong* journey. Not knowing the number of mu of their land and the income of their rural family was a frequent phenomenon among the migrant workers in their late teens and mid-twenties, both male and female. There was now a greater desire for them to look for possible ways to stay in the city. They understood that *dagong*, working for a boss, was not a long-term prospect, and now many more of them dreamed of turning themselves into bosses some day. The unfulfilled expectations and the incessant frustration of moving back and forth between the city and the country, as experienced by the second generation, inevitably create anger and grievances that cannot find release.

CONCLUSION

The reform has remade China and turned it into the workshop of the world. It has also remade a new politics of the Chinese working class. Taking a specific path of proletarianization, the second generation of peasant-workers has gradually become aware of their class position and participated in a series of collective actions. Having a quasi social status, *nongmin gong*, the second generation of migrant workers is now experiencing a deeper sense of anger and dissatisfaction than that of the first generation, accompanied by the realization that they are completely cut off – there is no return to their hometown. An "enclosure" has accompanied the unfinished process of proletarianization of Chinese peasant-workers, shaped by a spatial separation of production in urban areas and reproduction in the countryside.

We strive to make sense of the formation of the new Chinese working class, not only as a creation of the time, made only by social structure – the reform – but also as historical and political subjects who participated in making their social change – the great transformation of China into the workshop of the world. To the new Chinese working class, China becoming the workshop of the world was a lived experience. The lived experience imbued with anger, trauma, and the sense of unfairness in the lives of the second generation of peasant-workers is of tremendous significance in understanding the future development of class actions in China.

Xin's story was particularly highlighted, as it opened up a deeper understanding of the struggle in the workplace as well as in the rural setting. Xin's heart-rending experience is both individual and social, factory-based as well as communal. The politics of production and social reproduction were dialectically enacted and reinforced by each other. Xin is special only because he has a strong-minded father who tried his best to dash his son's dream of return. However, he is like many migrant workers who have tried and failed to establish a small business in their hometown. The failure forces them to leave the countryside again – an incessant, yet unfinished, process of proletarianization. A vicious circle has been created: the reform and the rural–urban dichotomy motivate a desire to leave the countryside; escape leads only to the hardship of factory life; the frustration of factory life induces the desire to return; however, there is no place for returning migrants – going out to *dagong* is considered the only means of survival and development. This vicious circle contributes to a series of brutally truncated life experiences, resulting, inevitably, in a politics of resentment. The migrant worker now has no hope and no vision that would provide meaning to a life of *dagong* in the factory of the world, leading to a search for an alternative that could allow escape from their existing life predicament.

5 Spatial Politics: Production and Social Production of the Dormitory Labor Regime

Recent studies of the expansion of global capitalism often center on the role of capital in general or the process of financialization in particular; at best, they provide an analysis of the capital–state nexus in the neoliberal turn at a time when the global economy is rapidly restructuring itself (Harvey 2007 [1982], 2010, 2014). In the study of the spatial politics of capitalism, jumping scales are often said to be achieved by the privilege of global capital with the assistance of the state. Together, global capital and the state create multiple scales of contradiction, which open up the space for resistance. While the enigma of capital in today's global capitalism is studied in detail, the dialectics of labor, if not displaced, is often taken as supplementary and undeveloped (Lebowitz 2003). Suffering from a Western-oriented view on the remaking of contemporary global capitalism and its incessant crisis based primarily on the function of capital, the contribution of the experiences of labor in the Third World to the shaping of the landscape of current capitalism has been seriously underplayed.

Drawing on ethnographic studies in the industrial towns and cities of China in the past decade, this chapter aims to bring "labor" and "class" back to the center of the spatial politics of global capitalism. In conceptualizing the dormitory labor regime as a form of spatial politics of labor, we argue that labor and its class, and its relation to capital and the state is central to the making of global production space. In our empirical studies, we see that the dormitory system embodies extraordinarily complex class contradictions that provoke workers' resistance to global capitalism through their daily and collective struggles along the lines of class, gender, and ethnicity. This chapter also highlights that class can be reactivated as a useful concept by rooting it in class experience from below, that is, in the everyday micro-politics of the dormitory labor regime, in which Chinese migrant workers are called upon to live out their own nuanced class experiences.

In the communal setting of a collective workers' dormitory in an industrial town in Shenzhen in the summer of 2013, I was amid a crowd of women workers who were chatting and watching a soap opera program on TV at the grocery store in their factory compound. It was an open area where most of the workers, without a family, from the rural areas of China, could spend their limited leisure time. This factory compound was gated, and inside the gate, five dormitory buildings were situated on the southern side of the company. While some of the women were rushing to take a shower or wash their clothes, others were enjoying the break from their overtime work. With no place to stay in the city where they sell their labor, the workers have to attach their accommodation closely to their employer or have the employer provide them with living space. The newly industrialized towns and cities in China featured impressive settings of workers' collective dormitories where one building can house a few thousand workers. On windy and chilly nights, the hanging clothes of the workers in the dormitory corridors were flying like colorful multinational flags. These were the flags of the new Chinese working class, symbolizing the borderlessness of capital and the wretchedness of the socialist earth.

China has been repositioned as the workshop of the world, sustained by a dormitory labor regime that ensures the new Chinese working class is remaking itself and reshaping its struggle at the core of global capitalism (Pun and Smith 2007). Along the axis of a variety of capitalisms in today's world, we argue that China, as the workshop of the world, is characterized by a "systematic" use of dormitory labor, irrespective of capital, industry, or individual. With increasingly complex class relations in contemporary China, the dormitory labor regime evolved to control and compress labor production and reproduction through different levels of spatialized labor. It also embodies extraordinarily complex class contradictions that invoke workers' resistance to global capitalism through their daily and collective struggles. In addition to the realm of production relations, the politics of daily reproduction generated by the dormitory labor regime is also a place of contestation.

The structural accounts of transnational production processes require a more micro but also deeper view of how the reconfiguration of spatial production influences the labor politics in a multi-scaled production site, where the macro-field of global economics meets the micro-field of local politics, labor market, gender relations, and workplace relations. In this chapter, we discuss a specific Chinese labor regime – the dormitory labor system which the lives of migrant workers are called upon to react to and resist. With a class and gender perspective, we understand this dormitory labor system as a unique form of labor use to fuel global production in newly industrialized regions of China.

WHAT IS A DORMITORY LABOR REGIME?

I met Mei in her dorm on the third floor of a dormitory building of a Disney supplier factory in Dongguan in the summer of 2005. In contrast to the first generation of women workers who wrote letters to their hometown family in the dorm, the new generation was now sending text messages via cell phone to their loved ones. Mei said, "The dorm is simply a place for sleep, there is hardly any life. But who cares? Not even the workers." The dorm room, which measured 30 square meters, was occupied by eight women, each of them having a bed space and a private locker, sharing a communal bathroom which was also the place for bathing. However, the setting was a real improvement compared with the living conditions of the first generation who were often housed in a dorm room of equal size but shared by more than 20 women. When they were not working, there was scarcely any place for Mei and her co-workers to go but their dorms, which were provided by their employer. Mei felt she had no freedom by keeping herself at the factory dormitory. For others, they preferred to stay in the nearby village apartments where the rent was often shared by four or five workers. In a similar way, all of them were also deprived of their normal life by this dormitory labor regime provided by capital.

A dormitory labor regime is characterized by the reconfiguration of daily production and reproduction space within a factory space in which work and residence are highly condensed in the same location. The political economy of providing accommodation close to the factory, linking space, state, and capital in channeling massive surplus labor from the countryside, certainly fuels global production (Pun and Smith 2007). As we have described, the migrant working class is deprived of citizenship rights in the city due to state control through the *hukou* system, and the meager income of this class pours oil on the flame. Because they have insufficient money to support housing costs in urban areas, workers have no choice but to take the temporary residence provided by their employer. To many China observers, China is a miracle, not only because of its rising economic power, but also because it has not turned into a "slum empire" by having 270 million migrant workers flowing in and out, between city and village, every year. What has absorbed this huge migrant working population? Why are there no slums in China's industrial cities as in most Third World societies undergoing rapid industrialization? The dormitory labor system provides a possible answer to this question. Extensively and systematically used in economic special zones and industrial towns, dormitories facilitate the temporary attachment or capture of labor by the companies, as working space and living space are highly integrated by capital and state. A transient workforce is created, circulating between urban and rural locations, and between factory and factory, allowing capital's control over living space and state control over residency permits. The dormitory labor regime is thus a hidden facsimile of the slums that were ubiquitous in most developing countries.

Gender is central to this specific embodiment of the Chinese dormitory labor regime and the formation of the transient working class. In the 1980s and 1990s, the first two decades of the exodus of internal migrant workers into the industrial cities, young and single women were among the first to be picked up by the new export-oriented industries. Often regarded as "submissive" and "obedient" laboring subjects with nimble fingers, young women constituted a high proportion of the factory workers, over 70 percent of the total workforce in garments, toys, and electronics industries who formed the first generation of Chinese migrant workers. Mostly aged between 18 and 25, these young and single women workers of the first generation were able to work as many as 14 hours a day, having no break on Sundays or Public Holidays. This was the prime time for capital as the new working class was still able to provide sufficient ideal labor, which was predominantly female.

Running into the 2000s, owing to the rapid expansion of capital accumulation in all sectors accompanied by a rapid increase of labor use, preferably women, the supply of female workers was all used up. There was a labor shortage, especially after 2004. Employers had been unwilling to take on male workers among the first generation of migrant workers, but eventually the factory gates were opened up to male workers, who were often considered unreliable or troublemakers, and then further opened up to married women and men, who were often viewed as not having enough youthfulness and energy to toil at work requiring day and night shifts. Today, because of a shortage of young labor in the newly industrialized towns and cities, both men and married female workers have become more of a target in garment, electronics, and toy enterprises, among many others. The second generation of migrant workers thus has a more balanced sex composition. Their gender, in addition to their youth and rural migrant status, is an integral part of China's export-led industrialism, facilitating global production for the world market. In the process of incorporating China into the global economy, we have seen an emergence of the dormitory labor regime, which embodies gendered *dagong* subjects, who live out their gendering process in this specific production space in China. It echoes a feminization of labor use in the expansion of global capitalism and the new international division of labor which combines with the micro gendering process in which the workers' gender identities are acquired (Ong 1987; Kondo 1990; Lee 1998; Pun 2005).

THE ORIGINS OF THE CHINESE DORMITORY LABOR SYSTEM

The dormitory labor system regime in China is not a new spatial fix occasioned by the reconfiguration of global capitalism. The dormitory use of labor has a long history both in a Western and Eastern context of industrialization (Pun and Smith 2007). In the pre-Liberation period, industrial dormitories were introduced by Japanese enterprises in the Shanghai region, which echoed the history of dormitory labor use in the period of rapid industrialization (Smith 2003). In developing countries such as South Africa, mining towns also extensively used industrial dormitories to house migrant male workers (Burawoy 1976, 1985). Western countries, Latin American countries, Japan, and Korea all used dormitory labor in the process of early industrialization.[1]

Looking into China's history, factory dormitories were first introduced in the early twentieth century on a limited scale when imperialism, as "a high stage form of capitalism" brought in foreign industrial capital. In a study of cotton and silk workers in Tianjin in the period from 1900 to the 1940s, Hershatter (1986) notes that dorms began to be introduced to lower labor costs through feminization and use of migrant workers in foreign-owned companies. Workers, however, were not willing to stay in company-provided dormitories if they had a choice to live with their relatives or co-villagers in nearby residential areas. As she points out,

> Had they been able to, the Tianjin mill owners would have made the factory a closed environment, serviced by company institutions and secured by company guards. But workers voted with their feet, resisting the attempt to turn housing into a "tool of discipline." (Hershatter 1986: 165)

Dormitories therefore became the preserve of single, rural women workers, those without family or local connections, and workers were prevented from leaving and were locked in at night (Hershatter 1986). In a similar study of female cotton workers in Shanghai in the 1930s, Emily Honig also notes that the contractors hired thugs to guard the dormitories and accompany women workers, even on their holidays and days off, and that women had to share beds, endure sexual abuse from contractors, overcrowding, and poor sanitation (1986: 106).

Elizabeth Perry, in her *Shanghai on Strike*, also says that the skilled artisans who made up the majority of Shanghai's first generation of industrial workers in pre-Liberation China,

> initially ... were required to live at the factory dormitory, but the number of employees quickly outgrew the 1500-person capacity of the dormitory, and many laborers moved into housing along Guangdong Road just outside the factory gates. Workers from the same distant geographical region living and working in such close proximity fostered a tightly knit immigrant community among Cantonese craftsmen at the arsenal. (1993: 36)

Perry argues that divisions among workers regarding their places of origin did not inhibit the growth of class consciousness, but through the networks formed in their shared dormitory setting and migrant community, workers' collective actions were nurtured. She records an insurgent role of an active early Chinese working class in Shanghai in pre-Liberation China.

In socialist China, state-owned enterprises in urban areas also provided accommodation to workers and their families but of an entirely different nature. These workers' families were often properly housed in an apartment unit by the state and hence the urban working class was considered the most privileged in China. The political economy of accommodation in socialist China was entirely different from that of the contemporary period in the way that the concept of socialist "units" acted as a commune providing permanent employment, housing, medical care, and education for the working class (Lu and Perry 1997). Today, the socialist "units" system has been totally shattered by the urban reforms which brought an end to the privileged Chinese working class that was built during the socialist period. Yet, what is strikingly changed about today's China is that through a combination of state controls (the *hukou* system), extensive provision of factory dorms by capital, and shortages of independent accommodation, the contemporary dormitory labor regime is more hegemonic, pervasive, and total than anything that existed in earlier periods of Chinese history or experienced by other workers in the Asian region. The dormitory labor system in today's China is unique in the way that dormitories are available to all workers and all industries, regardless of capital, sectors, and locations, and the widespread availability of industrial dormitories not only constrains the mobility of labor, it also facilitates it.

The new *dagong* subjects are not from the local or urban area where workplaces are based, but come as inter-provincial migrants for a temporary sojourn in a factory and are accommodated in dormitories. Their mobility is shaped by two social conditions: peasant-workers' "freedom" to sell their labor to global and private capital that has been allowed in post-socialist China, and state laws on population and mobility control that try to contain workers' freedom of mobility in order to meet the demands of transnational capital as well as China's urban development. Because of this double social conditioning, which is basically a paradoxical process, the freedom of the rural migrants to work in the industrial cities was checked by the social constraint preventing their permanent settlement and growth in the cities as a new force of the working class. The dormitory labor regime is hence the hybrid outgrowth of global capitalism combined with the legacies of state socialism that works to reconnect the sphere of production and daily social production to serve global capital accumulation.

IMAGING A MODERN DORMITORY REGIME

Let us enter a concrete and advanced garment factory to understand how a modern dormitory regime operates. We visited China Silver Garments the first time in 2003, and then revisited it ten years later in 2013. China Silver Garments is a joint venture company owned by a Chinese manager and a Taiwanese family entrepreneur in the Shanghai region. Established in 1995, the company was mostly under the control of the Mainland Chinese manager who was in charge of daily management and operation of the production, while the Taiwanese counterpart served to provide and secure production orders mainly from a big European corporation and Japanese buyers. China Silver Garments produces garments and underwear, using cloth bought and dyed in China. In addition to the European corporation and buyers in Asia, it also produces its own undergarment brand for the Chinese market.

Some 30 percent of China Silver Garments production went to the single European corporation, which then enforced a very strict company code of conduct on the factory. China Silver Garments had a high-end position along the global subcontracting chain. Owing to the contribution of Taiwanese capital, the company possessed direct contacts with the European buyer. Like the construction industry, garment production is also organized through a complex subcontracting system through a global supply and production chain. China Silver Garments subcontracted some of its orders, in particular the weaving process and some knitting activities, to local and smaller factories. While the management team was basically Mainland Chinese, China Silver Garments fostered an ambition to become the most advanced and modern enterprise in the Shanghai region, and which could live up to the required international standards. Using the local idiom, the Chinese manager said the goal was to let the company "go global." This was thought to ensure that the company would be able to survive and expand despite severe global competition by introducing modern management methods and international labor standards. The Chinese manager, a bright and ambitious figure, was keen on imagining a new paradigm of management for the Chinese workplace, which has long been associated with a "sweatshop" image internationally and locally.

The politics of spatial production in capital accumulation was explicitly important to China Silver Garments, concerned as it was for tapping into the circulation of global production. In March 2001, China Silver Garments moved into new premises close to Shanghai, built in a high-tech and development zone, newly planned as an export-processing zone for foreign, joint venture and private companies. The new compound appeared modern and sophisticated, consisting of a three-story building housing the production facilities, with an attached administrative block, a separate one-story canteen (with kitchen) and a detached utility room. The vast compound (some 18,000 square meters) had a substantial unoccupied area, where management planned to erect a modern dormitory with advanced facilities. Because of this new compound strategy, the proportion of ownership was skewed toward the Mainland Chinese manager who now had a 70 percent company share, while that of the Taiwanese counterpart has declined from 50 percent to 30 percent.

By 2003, when China Silver Garments already had an advanced company compound, what was lacking was a modern dormitory building that could meet SA 8000 requirements and the Corporate Code of the European buyer. Frequent inspections from the European corporation had hastened the process of building modern accommodation facilities for its workforce. Maintaining the number of employees at more than 1,000, a suitable size for retaining quality workers, the company aimed to maintain a relatively stable workforce, and a just-in-time labor system, which the on-site dormitory proffered, for a just-in-time production system. The task force said:

> The first priority is to build our dormitory as soon as possible. We need to meet the international requirements, but we also need to confine our workers in better living conditions so that they can be more accessible to work.

To keep the workers productive and prevent labor turnover seem to be the priorities of management from the above quote. The 'confinement' of the workforce in relatively good living conditions, under stricter management control, was paradoxically deemed a company strategy to retain workers who were often mobile and unreliable. The labor turnover rate in foreign or private-owned enterprises in China is particularly high, ranging between 30 and 90 percent each year (Smith 2003).

Labor mobility was a top concern not only for management, but also for the Chinese state when it has to deal with millions of rural migrants flooding the cities seeking job opportunities each year since the mid-1990s (see Cook 2002; Fan 2003). Ninety percent of the workforce in China Silver Garments were rural workers from villages or towns in Zhejiang and Jiangsu, two near-hinterland provinces of the Shanghai region. The remaining 10 percent were local workers who lived at home. More than 70 percent of the workers employed in China Silver Garments were women. Most were in their mid-twenties to mid-thirties. Accommodation of these workers thus was a sensitive problem for the company as the new dormitory provisions were still not ready.

The spatial hierarchy served to constitute a workforce hierarchy not only in terms of wage, work position, and status, but also living provisions (Rofel 1999). Global capitalism was built upon spatiality of differences and hierarchies, and was crystallized in the microforms of the labor process and dormitory provisions, at least in the transnational workplaces in China. The huge difference in accommodation provisions between the managerial staff, technical and clerical staff, and the production workers represented a spatial hierarchy that served to reinforce segmentation of the labor force. The company was renting flats and dormitory rooms in three different locations nearby. Two-bedroom flats were rented for managerial staff, forepersons, and office clerical staff whose living conditions were far better than production workers. A shared dining room, kitchen, toilet and bathroom with hot water facilities were provided in the flats. Dormitory rooms rented from government-built premises housing 8–16 workers were for production workers. Living conditions were generally poor and far from meeting the Corporate Code's requirements concerning minimum housing standards. No kitchen and bathroom were provided; a shared toilet used by more than 10 workers did not provide adequate sanitary conditions. Potable water was not provided to the workers, who had to buy it on the ground floor. Fire drills and emergency lighting were nonexistent and fire extinguishers were either completely absent or out of use.

Contrary to the Code, the workers were not provided with their own storage space for their clothes and personal belongings, which they had to hang over their beds. Generally, no fans were installed, even in the 16-bed double bunk dormitories on the upper floor of one building, where temperatures soared in summer. As hot water and showers were not available in some places, workers had to go to the public baths to get a shower, at a cost of RMB 5. Under pressure from the European corporation to adopt the Code, the management showed us a very sophisticated dormitory plan, which was drawn up by a construction and design company, based on the Code's requirements.

When we revisited China Silver Garments in 2013, the modern dormitory had long been built and used. It looked like a school building, with an open space on the ground floor, corridors on each upper floor, and very neat living rooms. Every room in the dormitory building now housed between four and six workers, providing an individual bed, lighting, storage space, and a shared kitchen, toilet, bathroom, fans, hot water facilities, and even air conditioners. A library, clinic, and recreational common room was located on the ground floor for all workers to use. With these accommodation facilities, the company expected to benefit by retaining a better quality workforce with more experience and skills for a longer period. However, even after several years, a dormitory with good facilities proved unable to help retain a stable workforce. The average length of tenure in China Silver Garments remains one or two years. Keeping a more stable and disciplined workforce is still at the top of the management's agenda. This aim of labor retention is somewhat contradictory given the young age profile of the workforce, and the relatively low wages reinforced by migrant labor circulation. "Longer term" attachment is therefore only for a few additional years and the migrant composition of labor is not expected to change. The additional welfare benefits within the factory compound are, as noted earlier, there to confine labor on a daily basis to better serve the needs of production and demands of the product market. A worker who had worked in China Silver Garments for more than three years told us:

> I am an old worker in this company. I came to this company because of its good working conditions, but gradually I realized that with this

small income, I have almost no hoping of bringing my family here. What's the use of a good-looking dormitory? It still keeps my family separated.

To many workers, this modern dormitory is not for the sake of workers, but to serve the inspection of transnational brands, which are interested in monitoring the working and living conditions with a checklist. Controlling the social, non-working lives of workers was envisioned as being possible through a modern dormitory space which is purposely designed and built. "More supervision and inspections can be enforced in the dormitory building, and women workers can be better protected," explained the facilities manager. He continued, "male workers won't be able to wander around in the streets at midnight, and smoking can be more effectively kept under control." Women and men are highly segregated in order to control sexual behaviors even though the living conditions of both genders are quite similar.

Self-management of dormitory rooms was also anticipated in that the workers would learn how to discipline themselves and maintain their living conditions properly. A modern dormitory regime with better living conditions thus meant a more subtle regime of surveillance over workers' bodies and subjectivities, along Foucauldian lines (Foucault 1977). In materialist terms, the larger the investment in the dormitory, the more management wanted to control it. A cleaner living place, more private and individualized space, and better ventilated rooms are all directed to constructing a modern and industrial being – a one-dimensional person suitable for producing high-class and world-famous garment brands. The price for these improved living conditions was a subtle surveillance system, in which the workers had to surrender their freedom of movement to the enhanced disciplinary power of management over their non-working lives.

China Silver Garments is not an exceptional case. As Chinese migrant workers amount to 90 percent of the total workforce, the issue of their housing conditions was, however, a touchy problem for management. In recent years more managements have replaced the system of fines for disciplinary reasons with a more positive system of reward programs. A modern dormitory labor regime was thus imagined and imaged by the managing director to live up to the age of globalizing production in a transnational context. This shows that one of the most common strategies of capital with regard to the dormitory labor regime is to accept the rationalization logic of transnational capital by embracing codes of conduct and international quality marks in order to access global markets.

THE DORMITORY LABOR REGIME AND THE NEW WORKING CLASS IN CHINA

The spectacle of China's urban industrial space is now shaped by the dormitory labor regime which has contributed to thousands and thousands of huge buildings temporarily used for housing peasant-workers. These production-cum-living spaces, disposable and replaceable, were meant to have a short life span, which shaped the transient nature of the working class. This transience, however, has become a permanent feature. While an individual dormitory building and an individual worker are present for only a short time, and transience is their nature, the expansion of dormitory space in almost all of the industrial towns and cities of China seems to be a trend. Since the establishment of the four Special Economic Zones in southern China in the early 1980s, these new export-oriented industrialized regions, dominated by foreign-invested enterprises, have relied heavily on dormitory labor. In the mid-1990s, these production spaces were rapidly expanded into the central and northern parts of China, where industrialized towns and cities were booming. Entering the 2000s, most of urban China was rapidly turning into the "workshop of the world," producing products labeled "Made in China" for domestic and overseas markets. As millions of migrant workers poured into industrial towns and cities, the provision of dormitories for the accommodation of these workers became a necessity for these enterprises. By reworking work and residential spaces, China's dormitory labor regime has been configured to facilitate the use of two generations of the new laboring class for the global accumulation of capital.

While there is a reified dormitory labor regime, we see a variation of dorm settlements in which enterprises manage their dormitory space. Let us take an industrial town in Shenzhen as an example.

1. *Enterprises rent dormitories*: Enterprises rent dormitories from the local government or local residents for their workers. This is the most common type and accounts for the majority of the industrial dormitories in Shenzhen, especially on the outskirts of industrial villages and towns. These enterprises are small- to medium-sized and usually have a workforce of more than a few hundred to a few thousand. The quality of this type of dormitory varies tremendously. A dorm room will be shared by eight to twelve persons, and the rent is usually 100 to 150 RMB per person each month in 2014, which may be inclusive or exclusive of utilities and other expenses. Washroom, bathing places, and drinking water facilities are all shared. Most of these enterprises provide a workers' canteen which is often subcontracted to a family-run small business.

2. *Enterprises own dormitories*: Large enterprises, especially transnational enterprises, often purchase land and build their own dormitory buildings. They are built by either local governments or private developers. These are large or transnational enterprises that have a workforce of several thousands and hence most of these plants own at least five or six dormitory buildings. Built like a hospital or a school, a room of 30 square meters will house eight to twelve persons. Accommodation is sometimes free of charge, while some enterprises will charge 100 RMB or more each month for

accommodation. Again, all living facilities have to be shared among workers. A common room is provided in large transnational companies.

3. *Workers rent dormitories*: Workers rent dormitories from the local residents in the village in the industrial town, because there are not enough rooms provided by their employers or because they are married. A room will cost as much as 500–600 RMB per month (in 2014) and will be shared by two to four persons. An apartment having three rooms will house six to twelve workers at the same time. These accommodation spaces will have a kitchen and dining room, but the workers are too busy to use them. Even though these spaces are rented by the workers themselves, none of them will treat the place like home, but rather, like the dorm, as a transient abode.

The variation and the complexity of these dormitory spaces, however, do not dilute the fact of the existence of this new working class: as rural subjects, their right of abode in the city is uprooted. Their fate as peasant-workers is embodied through this dormitory labor regime to which the simple and daily reproduction of labor is sustained in a very basic way. Attached to the factory's collective dormitories, the workers hand over their right of abode to the space of capital and create their own transience. As a peasant-worker, he or she is transient and disposable to capital, but this transience and disposability help subsume the value of his or her labor power continuously. Whenever and wherever the worker goes, the dormitory labor regime is waiting for him or her. No place to sleep in the city? No worry, the employer will give you a hand. As long as the wage of workers can be suppressed and is under the living costs in the city, the employer is more than happy to provide this help. Even though this dormitory labor regime is not intentionally constructed by capital, its result is a most productive and repressive space for extracting labor power and suppressing labor costs.

In most of the newly industrial towns, the Chinese state initially provides the factories with dormitory arrangements for the factory owners to rent. As housing provision is not for families, there is no interest from capital in the reproduction of the next generation of laborers. The focus is on maximizing the utilization of labor of the temporary, migrant, and contract laborers by controlling the daily reproduction of their labor power. Dormitories in China's foreign-invested manufacturing plants are communal multi-story buildings, and such living space is intensely collective, with no area available for even limited privacy, except the area within the closed curtains of a worker's bunk. But these physical conditions do not simply explain the role of the dormitory as a mode of production – as a living-at-work arrangement which creates double alienation for the workers.

Separated from family, from home, and from rural life, these workers are concentrated in a workspace and submit to a process of individuation as they are considered as "individual workers" by the management, unbound from communal bonds and responsible for their own behavior. And insofar as their connection to the firm is short-term and contractual, the alienation of labor derives from significantly more than either labor's separation from ownership of the product or labor's lack of production skills. Workers in dorms live in a system that alienates them from their past and that replaces a customary rural setting with factories dominated by unfamiliar others, languages, foods, production methods, and products (Smith and Pun 2006). The sense of alienation arises in both the realms of production and reproduction. If young Marx highlighted the embodiment of the sense of alienation in capitalist production relations, we add that the dormitory labor regime nurtures double alienation in the realm of reproduction by further cutting the workers' ties with their family, their village, and their communal bonds.

Hence, the subtle and multifaceted marginalization of a vast swath of the rural labor supply has created a precarious working class among

Chinese migrant workers. With the denial of the right to stay in the city, migrant workers must have employment first to be eligible for temporary residence. This denial further contributes to a deepening of class difference now, even with the relaxation of the *hukou* system, the workers, who receive wages that are below the cost of living, can hardly support their lives in the city. As a special form of state regulation of rural–urban migration (i.e., *hukou*), together with the control of migrant workers through the integrated working and living spaces (i.e., dormitories), the dormitory regime has successfully suppressed wage increases and lengthened working hours in the new urban industrial zones.

This is the secret of how China has been able to sustain a cheapening labor force for over two to three decades of rapid economic development. Take Foxconn as an example: as of May 2010, Foxconn paid 450,000 production line workers at its two Shenzhen plants – more than half of its total workforce in China – only 900 yuan a month for a 40-hour week. This subsistence level wage is not enough to meet workers' needs and compels workers to work up to 100 hours of overtime a month, close to three times the maximum 36 hours permitted by Chinese labor law (Article 41). In general, Chinese manufacturing wages as a percentage of US wages, compared to Japan and East Asian Tigers like South Korea and Taiwan at the beginning of their economic takeoffs, remained consistently low (Hung 2009).

In addition to the suppression of labor costs, the dormitory labor system also contributes to management of the foreign-invested or privately owned companies, which would appear to have exceptional control over the workforce under the system. With no access to a home space independent of the enterprise, working days are extended to suit production needs. This permits a flexible utilization of labor time, and means employers can respond to product demand more readily than in situations where workers' time is regulated by the state or workers themselves. If, as Marx noted in *Capital I*, the length of the working

day fluctuated within boundaries that are physical and social (1990
[1867]), then employers within this dormitory labor form would
appear to have massive control over "the social." Compared to the
"normal" separation between work and home that usual factory arrangements entail, the dormitory labor regime exerts greater breadth of
control into the working and non-working day of the workers.[2]

CONCLUSION

We would never deny the importance of capital in shaping the land-
scapes of global capitalism and its current crisis; however, we call for a
return of "labor" and "class analysis" to the centrality of the spatial politics of global capitalism with a Third World perspective. China, especially its role in shaping the global economy by providing a
200-million-strong internal migrant working class, provides valuable
non-Western experiences in reviewing the spatiality of current global
capitalism. Looking deeper into the dormitory labor regime, as a new
spatial politics of production, it serves as a base for China to rise as a
global factory driven by the globalization of capital accumulation and
transnational production. What is interesting here is that we see the
combination of the use of Taylorism and Fordism (mass assembly line,
mass political organization, and welfare-state interventions) with
various forms of flexible accumulation (flexible production, casual
labor, deregulation, and privatization through withdrawal of state
interventions). Taylorism, or the flexible production paradigm, alone
simply cannot explain the multiple spatiality of production in China.
In the Pearl River Delta we see thousands of foreign-invested companies which, if they employ one or two thousand workers, are considered small- to medium-sized plants. Mass assembly lines manned by
more than 10,000 workers for intensive production are now a norm in
garments, shoes, toys, and electronics industries, to name just a
few. In the Yangtze River Delta, we can easily find a single factory

compound hiring more than 10–15,000 workers, and yet this factory can at the same time hook up with a bunch of family workshops using only one or two laborers. A highly complex mode of production intersecting traditional Taylorist methods with various flexible production regimes is now dominated by the use of dormitory labor.

Hence, what is emerging is the transnational political economy of production that links not only to a new scale of the economic, but a new economy of scale, in which a multiple spatialized labor force is extensively manipulated for capital accumulation on a global dimension (Pun and Smith 2007). Under this spatial arrangement, Chinese dormitory labor stands out as the most efficient and dominant capital strategy that fits nicely with just-in-time global production. Apple, Disney, Samsung and many other brands can now secure their "zero-stocking" retailing strategy by requesting their supplier factories to provide "just-in-time" products. By using the dormitory labor regime in production, where working and living spaces merge, a great mass of workers can easily be ordered to work flexibly and in a prolonged way, reflecting the changing global business practices. The defining nature of the dormitory labor system is that both work and residence are closely combined, and production and daily social reproduction are reorganized for the sake of global capital use, with daily reproduction of labor entirely controlled by foreign-invested or privately owned companies.

In short, this dormitory labor regime, though in various forms, sustains a transient migrant workforce and an incomplete process of proletarianization that has affected the formation of the new working class in China. After all, this is the structural base – a transformed and transforming spatial politics that interprets the politics of the new working class in today's China.

In this sense, the struggles of the new migrant working class, which are manifold, heterogeneous and multi-sited, can no longer be described or politicized as officially pronounced "class struggles," as the subjects experience, make sense, react, and project their life trajectories in contemporary China. This does not mean that class analysis is simply outdated as the language of class is now diluted by the hegemonic discourses of the state and capital in the search for a "globalized" China. As a weapon of social struggle, class analysis, if useful, can only be reactivated by rooting it in class experience from below, that is, in the everyday micro-politics of the dormitory labor regime in which the Chinese workers themselves are in confrontation with capitalism and the market. The new Chinese worker- subjects have to live out their own class experiences as part of their life struggles in concrete living spaces. Face-to-face sharing of worries, exchanging feelings of a sense of a limited future, sharing of common anger and frustration, and planning organized actions make the confrontation of abstracted capital possible. The spatial proximity of production and reproduction sites nurtures the formation of new class subjects, albeit with great difficulties. The new worker-subjects that have emerged at the intersection of global capitalism and the Chinese modernity project invoke a desire for a return to "class analysis" at the workers' dormitory, a space where the workers live out their own complexities and their conflictual life experiences.

<table>
<tr><td>6</td><td>Monopoly Capital in China: The Foxconn Experience and Chinese Workers</td></tr>
</table>

Monopoly Capital in China: The Foxconn Experience and Chinese Workers

INTRODUCTION

In 2010, a startling 18 young migrant workers attempted suicide at Foxconn Technology Group production facilities in China, 14 of whom died, while four survived with injuries.[1] All were between 17 and 25 years of age – in the prime of their youth. Chinese media has dubbed the tragedy the "suicide express" (Pun and Chan 2012). This chapter looks into the new development of monopoly capital in global industrial capitalism and its impact on the factory system and factory life in China. It also illustrates how the state helps facilitate industrial production expansion as a form of monopoly capital by means of rapid concentration and centralization of capital on an unimaginable scale (Braverman 1998). Foxconn stands out as a prime example of this new phenomenon of capital concentration and centralization because of its speed and scale of capital accumulation in all regions of China that is incomparable to other enterprises. As the world's largest electronics factory, Foxconn ate up a huge number of small factories in the same sector not only in China, but also other parts of the world, spreading its facilities and offices over more than 30 countries. Unprecedented in history and without compare globally, Foxconn now has 1,400,000 staff and workers in its industrial empire and is the sole manufacturer for Apple and other brands. Working under this monopoly capital, Chinese workers were enticed to work in a global top 500 company, but nevertheless were subjected to such work pressure that their desperation might lead to suicide on the one hand, but also open up daily and collective resistance on the other.

The existing literature has argued that China's rise is a state-driven globalization process in which the state has facilitated export-led growth relying primarily on joint venture and wholly-owned foreign capital (Huang 2003, 2008; Guthrie 2012). China's heavy reliance on foreign direct investment during the past decades, far more extreme than the East Asian countries during their industrial takeoff, has brought about high-speed economic growth but also widened labor and social inequality and environmental deterioration (Davis and Wang 2009; Solinger 2009; Perry and Selden 2010). The peculiar proletarianization process of Chinese internal migrant workers helps lower not only production costs, but also social reproduction costs in host cities. Similar to other foreign-invested companies in China, Foxconn has largely benefited from the state-driven globalization process and the unique process of proletarianization, as it enjoyed preferential policies offered by local governments and cheap production and labor costs when it moved its production bases from Taiwan to Mainland China in the late 1980s. It also made use of the structure of the rural–urban divide, the gender and class differences that made up the dreams and pursuits of rural laboring subjects in the age of consumerism.

The suicides of Foxconn workers who produced iPhones and iPads alarmed the world. Sparked by the spate of suicides and subsequent worker struggles, in June 2010, we began to collaborate with faculty and students from 20 universities in Mainland China, Taiwan and Hong Kong to investigate Foxconn's labor management and factory practices. Over these five years, researchers from Peking University, Tsinghua University, Taiwan National University, Taiwan Tsinghua University, Chinese University of Hong Kong, Hong Kong Polytechnic University, and many others have conducted extensive fieldwork in Shenzhen, Wuhan, Kunshan, Shanghai, Zhengzhou, Chengdu,

Chongqing, Taiyuan, and Langfang. This is probably the first time that sociologists from Greater China and the international university community have come together to conduct joint research, sharing concerns about the lives and struggles of China's new working class through the lens of Foxconn and its relationship to Apple in our global economy. In surveys of 3,000 people that we conducted in Shenzhen, Zhengzhou, Chengdu, and Chongqing, the average age of Foxconn respondents was 21.1, the youngest 15. To supplement our structured questionnaires, we have documented workers' narratives and field observations to present the working and everyday lives of the young Foxconn employees. Our primary concern is the dominating mode of corporate management and its impacts on workers' well-being.

Against this background, this chapter begins with a story of a woman worker, Ou Yang, who was working hard and dying to own an iPhone. When consumers across the globe face a dizzying array of choices in the latest electronics gadgets, China's young workers who actually produce these goods are just as eager to buy them as Western consumers. Ou Yang, a 19-year-old Foxconn worker, talked about her future. "Someday," she mused, "I want to drive a brand new Honda and return home in style!" For the time being, she dreamed of buying an iPhone, and she would work as hard as necessary to do so.

Yang was born in a "traditional village" in central China's Hubei province. The most important event for every household was the birth of a son. After giving birth to a son, a family could hold its head high; those who did not have a son were mocked or even bullied. When Yang's mother was pregnant yet again, the entire family was brimming with expectations. But her mother give birth to another girl! Her father was so disappointed he sulked all day. Her grandmother, anxiously awaiting a grandson to embrace, refused to give a name to the new child. Later, the family's hopes were shattered as Yang's mother gave birth to two more baby girls in desperately trying to produce a male heir.

When mother was young she was very beautiful, which is why my father married her. Not long after they married, father always listened to her. But after she gave birth to four girls in a row, mother no longer had status in the family. So then he took control of the family, and in our household my father's word is final. Now he treats mother badly, even beating her.

Yang cultivated a strong, rebellious personality. She said: "I want the whole village to know, the girls in our family are extraordinary!" Her desire for independence and freedom fused in her dream to own an iPhone. Working for Foxconn seemed one step closer to making her dream a reality.

After graduating from middle school in her home town, Yang hoped to enter a vocational school in Wuhan, the provincial capital of Hubei, to study photography, but her parents refused. Money was tight. At that time, her father had a business selling building materials, but he did not earn much. Having all four sisters in school at the same time was a great financial burden. Whenever Yang thought about asking her parents for money, she felt ashamed. "I felt as if I was one of my parents' debts."

In a fit of anger, Yang left home to work, determined to become independent. With her still childish face and a book bag on her back, Yang showed up at a garment factory in Shanghai where her cousin worked. Taking on an apprenticeship, she received only 400 yuan per month as living expenses for the first three months. It was the summer of 2008.

Yang worked in the small garment factory for a year, "each day consisting of one assembly line and three points – dormitory, factory, and cafeteria – life was pure and simple." Finally one day, she grew weary. In this kind of life, "aside from the weather changing outside the window, nothing changes," she thought.

But as if a restless spirit had crept into her body, Yang began to look forward to changing her life. She left the garment factory and went to work at Foxconn's Kunshan factory. Yang was dressed more fashionably than most other workers, wearing a dropped waist, knee-length skirt. She made great efforts to improve her income and skills by moving between jobs.

In the future, Yang plans to settle in the big provincial city of Wuhan, thinking above all of helping her mother:

> We can get up at 6 every morning hand in hand and walk in the park, come back at 7 or 8 and have breakfast, then sit on rocking chairs holding a fan, chitchatting, at night eat some watermelons, watch some television. Mother said that if she is able to live like this for just a while she will be satisfied. She has had only two hopes in life, one is to live a life of ease like this; the other is to visit Tiananmen Square in Beijing to see the flag raising ceremony. I don't think it's hard! I can help her make it happen.

Yang, like many other workers, has a dream of a better future by improving the living conditions for her family, and returning home with an iPhone in her back pocket. To achieve this, she has had to give herself over to Foxconn, which has captured her labor power and that of other ambitious subjects over the past two decades. Yang's story is a reflection of Foxconn's growth in China, which demonstrates a new phenomenon of capital expansion in terms of the size of workforce, the scale of factory compounds, and the number of factories dotted over the map of the country.[2] Having a total workforce of over one million in China, Foxconn has grown to be a mega-workshop of the world, with a single factory compound employing an extraordinary number of workers, ranging from 100,000 to over 400,000. Foxconn has become a form of monopoly capital and it now dominates the world market by producing 50 percent of the world's electronic products.

FOXCONN: THE ELECTRONIC WORKSHOP OF THE WORLD

Hon Hai Precision Industry Company, more commonly known by its trade name Foxconn, was founded in Taipei in 1974. The name "Foxconn" alludes to the corporation's ability to produce electronic connectors at nimble fox-speed. Foxconn is currently the world's largest contract manufacturer of electronics, providing "6C" products – computers (laptops, desk-tops, tablet personal computers such as iPads), communications equipment (iPhones), consumer products (digital music players, cameras, game consoles, TVs), cars (automotive electronics), content (e-book readers such as Kindle), and healthcare products.[3] The corporate annual revenue reached an all-time high at 2.9972 trillion Taiwan New Dollars for the year 2010 (approximately US$95.2 billion), with a year-on-year increase of 53 percent.[4]

Foxconn has evolved into a global industrial leader in three stages. The first stage was to advance into Mainland China under the coastal development strategy in the early reform period. Shenzhen Special Economic Zone (SEZ), at the northern border of Hong Kong, opened to Western and Asian capital investment in 1980. Local officials provided overseas investors with a wide array of preferential policies, including tax exemptions, cheap land costs, and streamlined procedures for speedy export. In 1988, Foxconn set up its first offshore factory in Shenzhen, with a small workforce of 150 internal migrant workers from the countryside in Guangdong Province, of whom some 100 were women workers.[5] The first floor of the all-in-one factory compound was a canteen, the second to fifth floors the production lines, and the sixth floor the collective dormitory for the Chinese assembly workers. In contrast, the Taiwanese expatriates lived in rental

apartments in the manufacturing town. In the early stage of production, middle- and high-level management was controlled by the
Taiwanese.

During the 1990s, in its second stage of expansion, Foxconn greatly
benefited from the cheap supply of internal migrant labor as it
demanded more human resources. It required the specialization of
labor and the diversification of production lines. It also employed an
increasing number of skilled Chinese staff and workers in low- to
mid-level management. By the turn of the twenty-first century,
Foxconn had consolidated its production clusters in two regions:
the Pearl River Delta in the south and the Yangtze River Delta in
the east, where local state governments in places such as Shenzhen,
Shanghai, and Kunshan provided businesses with preferential tax
policies, land and industrial infrastructure, and substantial labor supplies (Hsing 1998).

The third and latest stage of Foxconn's expansion is the building of
monopoly capital by mergers and relocation of production facilities
across all regions in China. Since the early 2000s, Foxconn tapped into
the lower-cost labor and infrastructural resources in northern, central,
and western regions. As early as 2002, CEO Terry Gou was crowned
"the king of outsourcing" by *Bloomberg Businessweek* (Culpan 2012),
when Foxconn was still behind longstanding industry leaders Solec-
tron and Flextronics. In the same year, the company became China's
leading exporter. As of December 2008, Foxconn's global sale revenues
reached US$61.8 billion.[6] As consumer demand for electronic goods
rose following the recovery from the 2008–9 global financial crisis,
Foxconn jumped to 30th place – from 60th previously – in the 2014
Global 500 corporate listing, marking a significant 60.5 percent increase
in revenues to an unprecedented high of US$132 billion.[7] Foxconn
integrates production chains from raw material extraction to final
assembly to reduce market uncertainties and enhance cost and time
effectiveness. Through mergers and acquisitions as well as strategic

partnerships, Foxconn is able to shorten its downstream supply chain by manufacturing some parts in-house. Spokesman Arthur Huang explained the company's cost-saving method:[8]

> We either outsource the components manufacturing to other suppliers, or we can research and manufacture our own components. We even have contracts with mines which are located near our factories.

Subject to the iron laws of capitalist production that force the individual capitalist to compete with others in the market, Foxconn has intensified its race for new business. It made desktop and tablet computers and laptops, fighting for orders against specialized Taiwanese manufacturers such as Quanta Computer, Compal Electronics, and Wistron. In order to secure production orders from leading technology brands such as Samsung Electronics, Hewlett-Packard (HP), Sony, Apple, Microsoft, Dell, and Nokia, Foxconn has widened its product portfolio and upgraded its technology to bid for future business (Hurtgen et al. 2013). By mid-to-late 2011, Foxconn was projected to capture more than 50 percent of the world market share in electronics manufacturing and services.[9]

"In 20 years," business executives have suggested, "there will be only two companies – everything will be made by Foxconn and sold by Wal-Mart."[10] Exaggerated somewhat, but it does underline the impressive industrial growth of Foxconn in the Chinese and global economy. Indeed, China is a key geopolitical site for Foxconn, hosting in excess of one million Foxconn manufacturing workers, that is, a number far greater than its total workforce in all other countries where Foxconn has investment.[11] Foxconn's China operation has also extended from production to retail sales.[12]

Our interview data shows that the influx of rush orders has pushed Foxconn production workers to their physical and psychological limits, leading to workers' suicides as well as individual and collective resistance at the workplace. In the next section, we analyze Foxconn domination in relation to the Chinese state's strategy of wealth accumulation and more balanced coastal and inland developments. These shifts in state policies have shaped the working lives of the new generation of rural migrant workers.

THE CHINESE STATE AND LOCAL ACCUMULATION

Foxconn's achievement as a big-name electronics contract manufacturer is an important factor, making possible China's emergence as the workshop of the world and the second largest economy in the world. Building on the foundation of heavy industrial growth during the state socialist era from the 1950s to late 1970s, Chinese reformers moved to initiate market reforms and emphasize light industry and services. Asian-invested and domestic firms have gained economic support from the government, varying by region, to become suppliers to Western technology multinationals through exports in the 1990s through to the present (Leng 2005; Hung 2009; Appelbaum 2011).

The Chinese national economy has thus been fundamentally transformed from a heavy industry based on guaranteed lifetime employment and high welfare provided to urban workers, to one that relies mainly on foreign and private investments and massive use of migrant laborers in light industries, where labor costs and labor protections have been severely suppressed. The post-socialist state has further controlled workers' self-organization and consequentially wages to facilitate low-cost exports (Pringle 2013). Throughout the decades of rapid light industrialization, the manufacturing wages of the Asian Tigers rose from approximately 8 percent of US wages in 1975 to over 30 percent in the 1990s through 2005; by contrast, China's manufacturing wages over the years from 1980 to 2005 remained fairly low at approximately 2–3 percent of US wages (Hung 2008: 162). Despite important measures to increase legal minimum wages from the mid-2000s, social divisions and class inequalities have been widened.

As monopoly capital further expands, the concentration of capital vertically led to spatial expansion of production horizontally. Foxconn facilities in the coastal areas have been shifting inland, driven by rising production costs and inflation, the shortage of labor in coastal China, and the government's strategy to open its interior. The State Council has approved plans for the Cheng-Yu Economic Zone (*Cheng-Yu Jingji Qu*, that is, Chengdu and Chongqing), a regional project to link up the economic development between the two cities of Chengdu and Chongqing, in order to further boost the economy of western China. With the encouragement of the central government, local government leaders promote the export-oriented growth model by creating a business-friendly environment on the one hand, and reverse the historical trend of labor out-migration by improving local employment on the other. Meanwhile, young workers and married migrants have increasingly taken the job opportunities opened up in their native locations instead of moving to distant provinces. Government statistics for 2013 showed that while eastern China is still the primary preference for out-going rural migrant workers because of its relatively higher wages, eastern, central, and western China have narrowed the gap: more than 49.36 million migrants worked in the east region, around 64.24 million in the central region, and nearly 52.50 million in the western region.[13] While Foxconn Chongqing and Foxconn Chengdu were able to recruit laborers from their respective territories, most of the "local workers" were rural migrants from the countryside who had to commute for at least a few hours to their workplaces and were not able to go home on their day off at the weekends.

In short, Foxconn, like other leading investors, is moving energetically to take advantage of lower wages and local government incentives to build new production facilities in central and western regions. There

Figure 6.1: Foxconn production facilities in China, Hong Kong, and Taiwan
Source: Foxconn Technology Group company websites.

are over 30 Foxconn factories across Mainland China (in some cities Foxconn operates more than one production facility) (see figure 6.1).

Local inland governments engage in business partnership with Foxconn by providing it with access to land resources, roads and railways, bank loans, and labor under their jurisdiction. In order to promote the "go west" strategy and the post-2008 earthquake reconstruction program, Sichuan provincial and Chengdu city officials led a delegation to Foxconn's headquarters in Taiwan to sign a memorandum of cooperation in June 2009. Chinese officials promised to facilitate the relocation of more industries to the west, making possible formation of an efficient supply chain network like those previously created in Guangdong and in the Greater Shanghai area. A vice director of the Chengdu Hi-Tech Zone recalled:[14]

> There was a great deal of negotiation involved over the last five years before we got his [Foxconn CEO Terry Gou] investment. It was not easy for Chengdu to stand out in those cities vying for investment.

The Sichuan government leaders prioritized the construction of a Foxconn production complex and dormitories as the "Number One Project". The US$2 billion Foxconn investment project is the biggest to date in the province. As of the summer of 2010, a total of 14 villages in Deyuan town had been demolished to create the 15-square-kilometer industrial space designated for a comprehensive Foxconn Living Zone (that is, approximately five times larger than the flagship Foxconn Longhua factory in Shenzhen). During our field observation in March 2011 and summer of 2013, we learned that the township and village governments have offered free labor recruitment services for Foxconn Chengdu. A Sichuan worker vividly commented:

> Foxconn is hiring, the whole city has gone crazy too. Local officials grab people and ask if they'd be suitable to go work at Foxconn. The government has made it an official task. Officials at each level have a recruitment quota. Is this recruitment not crazy?

At the government buildings of the towns of Hongguang and Pi Tong, for example, the human resources officers directly assisted walk-in job applicants to arrange interviews at Foxconn. These services, made available since Foxconn Chengdu commenced its production in the third quarter of 2010, have greatly lowered corporate recruitment costs.

Moreover, Sichuan leaders have waived Foxconn a "significant" amount of rent and tax regarding the expanding investment projects. The renovated "northern plant" in the Chengdu Export Processing

Zone and the completely new or still-under-construction "southern plant" in the Chengdu Hi-Tech Industrial Development Zone are provided for Foxconn at "far below market rate." It is not surprising that Foxconn CEO Terry Gou praised the government for its cooperation,[15]

> [I'm] very much impressed by the efficiency of local government departments that led to the start of the project … Foxconn will add investment to make the [Chengdu] factory one of Foxconn's key production bases in the world.

Perhaps a more significant finding is the "dispatch" of students from vocational schools to work in surveyed Foxconn factories through the mediation of education officers of respective local governments in Wuhan, Chengdu, Chongqing, Shenzhen, Kunshan, Langfang, and Taiyuan (Pun and Koo 2014; Pun et al. forthcoming). Student interviewees reported to us that education departments and government officers-in-charge have "requested" their schools to arrange internships at Foxconn factories. Under China's Education Law, students who carry out internships organized by their schools maintain a student identity at all times. Student interns do not receive the protection of the Labor Law because their relationship with the work organization is not defined as employment. As the students are not the target of Labor Law regulations, conflicts that arise between the students and the work organization cannot be handled as labor disputes. As the students are not defined as laborers in the legal sense, they do not enjoy trade union membership either (Perlin 2011).

Hence we found that student workers at Foxconn with internships organized collectively by their schools have become an enormous worker community in Foxconn factories across the country. The majority of student interns we encountered came from their second or third year of study, and most were 16 to 18 years of age. Despite the maximum eight-hour work day stipulated by Education Ministry regulations, the intern workers at Foxconn frequently did excessive overtime work during the day or night shift. Many students complained:

> I feel that what I've learned in my major is of no use; I've used nothing here.

> Regardless of your major you are asked to do things they want, there is no relation to what you study in school.

> We don't learn any technical skills at Foxconn, every day is just a repetition of one or two simple motions, like a robot.

Foxconn's "student internships" are actually a way of implementing "student labor," to help raise output and increase profits by paying sub-minimum wages during the busy season. Foxconn exploits legal loopholes that do not require them to sign a formal labor contract for the use of student workers. The labor cost is further reduced as student interns, unlike their fellow migrant workers, are not entitled to government-run social insurance schemes (as they are not protected under the labor laws and regulations). In all these ways, Foxconn's labor regime – characterized by tight control of workers and super-exploitation of students – contributes to its rapid capital accumulation.

In short, the dominance and monopoly of Foxconn, we argue, is achieved through the dismantling of the socialist economy by the reform and open-door policy in general and a deepening engagement between local states and monopoly capital in particular over recent years. Local states compete fiercely to host a Foxconn production base to enhance economic growth, offering lucrative resources to the technology giant. A huge network of electronics manufacturing coordinated by Foxconn is thus fast expanding across geographic spaces on Mainland China. Inside the Foxconn "Empire," management organizes labor processes through a highly centralized and hierarchical production system, in which the workforce is subjected to a panoptic discipline, resulting in workers' suicides and resistance.

MIGRANT WORKERS IN THE FOXCONN "EMPIRE"

We are extremely interested in understanding the hidden abode of production of an example of monopoly capital and how Foxconn manages to "rule" over its million-strong workforce. A Foxconn "Empire" – as the workers often call it – is a distinctive dormitory factory regime which organizes spheres of production and reproduction. Foxconn's biggest manufacturing campus, Shenzhen Longhua, once with a workforce of more than 400,000 in 2010 and 2011, has currently dropped to less than 200,000 workers due to factory relocation and expansion in inland China. This 2.3-square-kilometer campus includes: factories, warehouses, 12-story dormitories, a psychological counseling clinic, an employee care center, banks, two hospitals, a library, a post office, a fire brigade with two fire engines, an exclusive television network, an educational institute, bookstores, soccer fields, basketball courts, track and field facilities, swimming pools, cyber theaters, supermarkets, a collection of cafeterias and restaurants, and even a wedding dress shop. This main campus is divided into 10 zones, equipped with first-class production facilities and the "best" living environment, as it is the model factory for customers, central- and local-level governments, and visitors from media organizations and other inspection units. In the same city of Shenzhen, another production campus, called Guanlan, housing over 100,000 workers, has none of the "additional" facilities of Longhua, consisting exclusively of multi-story factories and high-rise dormitories that are quite common to other foreign-owned companies.

In the Foxconn Group, the production lines on the factory floor are centrally administered by their respective departments or sections, which are directly responsible for their business units, business

* Currently, there are 15 Business Groups in Foxconn.

Figure 6.2: Foxconn production organization
Source: data from Foxconn Technology Group (2010).

divisions, and ultimately business groups (see figure 6.2). At present, there are in total 15 Foxconn business groups, differentiated by product specialization and/or corporate customers.

Foxconn competes on "speed, quality, engineering service, efficiency, and added value" to maximize profits. Its 12-level management hierarchy with clear lines of command is organized in a pyramid; in the chain of layers in the workshop alone, frontline workers face multiple layers of management from assistant line leaders, line leaders, team leaders, and supervisors (see figure 6.3). There is a broad three-tiered incentive scheme at Foxconn: at the upper stratum are decision-making leaders who are rewarded by company share dividends and job tenure for their loyalty, commitment, and seniority; at the middle level are managing and supervisory staff who are rewarded by housing and monetary benefits; and on the lower rung are ordinary workers whose wages and welfare are barely minimal.

The labor process in Foxconn is organized by a hierarchical management principle. Division of labor is so detailed that workers see themselves as merely "a cog in the machine." Senior managers formulate

CEO
Vice presidents
General managers
Associate general managers
Directors
Managers
Associate managers
Supervisors
Team leaders
Line leaders
Assistant line leaders
Production operators & student interns

Figure 6.3: Levels of management in Foxconn
Source: based on Foxconn Technology Group (2010).

strategic plans and rules and standards and the lower-level staffers have to execute them at the lowest cost to achieve the greatest efficiency. Foxconn production operators in general do not require "skill" or thought; and only strict implementation of instructions from management and mechanical repetition of each simple movement is required.

CORPORATE CULTURE

"Low tech, high tech, making money is tech," says Terry Gou, the CEO and founder of Foxconn, a saying taken from "Gou's Quotations," a document that company managers are expected to read and remember. This pragmatic approach is strikingly similar to that of reformist leader

Deng Xiaoping: "White cat, black cat, if it catches mice it is a good cat." "Gou's Quotations" evoke collective memories of the older generation of people who came of age during the collective era and recited "Mao's Quotations" in political campaigns and in schools. In the Taiwanese-invested firm, when Foxconn staff test for promotion, some of the test questions are to write "Gou's Quotations" from memory. Several famous examples are:

> A harsh environment is a good thing.
> Suffering is the identical twin of growth.
> Outside the lab, there is no high-tech, only execution of discipline.

"No admittance except on business" – every Foxconn factory building and dormitory has security checkpoints with guards standing by 24 hours a day. In order to enter the shop floor, workers must pass through layers of electronic gates and inspection systems. Workers repeatedly expressed the feeling that the entry access system made them feel as if working at Foxconn is to totally lose freedom:

> We are not allowed to bring cell phones or any metallic objects into the workshop. They are confiscated. If there is a metal button on your clothes or necklace, it must be removed, otherwise you won't be allowed in, or they [security officers] will simply cut the metal button off.

While getting ready to start work on the production line, management will ask the workers: "How are you?" Workers must respond by shouting in unison, "Good! Very good! Very, very good!" This militaristic drilling is said to train workers as disciplined laborers. Production quotas and quality standards are passed down through channels to the frontline workers on the lowest level of the pyramid.

Workers recalled how they were punished when they talked on the line, failed to catch up with the high speed of work, and made mistakes in work procedures. Several women workers attaching speakers to MP3-format digital audio players said:

> After work, all of us – more than 100 persons – are made to stay behind. This happens whenever a worker is punished. A girl is forced to stand to attention to read aloud a statement of self-criticism. She must be loud enough to be heard. Our line leader would ask if the worker at the far end of the workshop could hear clearly the mistake she has made. Oftentimes girls feel they are losing face. It's very embarrassing. Her tears drop. Her voice becomes very small…Then the line leader shouted: "If one worker loses only one minute [failing to keep up with the pace of the work], then, how much more time will be wasted by 100 people?"

Line leaders, who are also under pressure, treat workers harshly to reach productivity targets. The bottom line for management is daily output, not workers' feelings. Workers, in return, made fun of their line leaders in their daily life by mocking Foxconn's "humane management" as "human subordination". A male worker sharply commented:

> If someone makes a mistake at Foxconn, the person below them must take responsibility. If something bad happens I get screwed, one level screws another…higher level people vent their anger at those below them, but who can workers vent to? That's why frontline workers jumped from those buildings.

Factory-floor managers and supervisors often give lectures to production workers at the beginning and the end of the work day. After working a long shift of a standard 12 hours (in which four hours are overtime), workers still have to stand often for 15 minutes to half an hour and listen to speeches, although the content of such meetings remains the same: the management evaluates the production target of the previous shift, reminds workers of the tasks they need to pay special attention to, and work rules and regulations. Workers know too well that branded electronic products are expensive and there is no margin for mistakes. Several workers at the mobile phone assembly workshop commented:

> We get yelled at all the time. It's very tough around here. We are trapped in a "concentration camp" of labor discipline – Foxconn manages us through the principle of "obedience, obedience and absolute obedience!" Must we sacrifice our dignity as people for production efficiency?

Despite the attempt to take panoptic control over the workers on the production line, we found that the workers, in agony, would resist management in a variety of ways including daily and collective resistance: stealing products, slow-downs, stoppages, small-scale strikes, and sometimes even sabotage, which put back production badly. During our research, Foxconn workers informed us from time to time that if they could not endure their management on the line, they would take concerted action and worked as slow as possible in order to embarrass their line leaders. Once the workers won a small victory by having their line leader changed because this line leader was too harsh to them; in another instance, everybody stopped working on the line when the production order was too much of a rush, gaining managerial concessions. In short, there are inevitable tensions and resistances built in to the repressive regime of Foxconn, despite its hype of harmony and "mutual love and care."

WAGES AND WORK HOURS

"Heart to heart, Foxconn and I grow together," reads a bright red banner hanging at the new factory in Foxconn Chengdu. It suggests the identification of workers and the company with one big heart. The corporate propaganda team has created a dream of riches through labor and tried to persuade workers that success and growth is only possible through diligently working.

As of March 2014, the basic monthly wage (for a 40-hour normal work week) for assembly-line workers was 2,450 yuan (or US$375) in Foxconn Shenzhen, with all the other nine surveyed Foxconn factories falling around this figure, depending on geographical location. All the workers and student interns interviewed had "agreed" to do overtime to earn more money, totaling 3,000–3,500 yuan a month. The wage rates of average workers at Foxconn generally are a little bit higher than the national pattern: in 2013 the average wages of the 166 million out-going migrant workers (including overtime) were estimated at 2,609 yuan a month.[16] So the complaints of Foxconn workers are not illegal underpayment of wages but the perceived huge gap between themselves and their higher level managers as well as the salaried people in the cities.

"*Fushikang,* The People of Foxconn," literally translated, means "wealthy" and "healthy" people, which has a dark irony for many "Foxconn People" we talked to. The Foxconn workers often took this phrase as a joke when they received their monthly wage. Regarding his present meager wages, one 25-year-old worker – at his marriageable age – expressed anxiety about his future life, and especially about having a family:

> I'm no longer able to muddle along at my job in Shenzhen, every month I make only over a few thousand yuan, and if I don't marry I could get by for a few years, but if I marry, I will have to raise kids, it's really not enough for that…Our days are truly hectic, and even if you are strong it is difficult. Most people in my dorm are unmarried, and I feel that married people generally won't come here, the wages are low.

PRODUCTION INTENSITY AND WORK PRESSURE

Workers reported that, after the basic wage increase to 1,200 yuan in June 2010, a clear increase in production was scheduled and production intensity increased. A group of young workers at the Shenzhen Guanlan factory responsible for processing cell phone casings said:

> The production output was set at 5,120 pieces per day in the past but it had been raised by 20 percent to 6,400 pieces per day in recent months. We were completely exhausted.

The biggest Longhua factory could produce as many as 137,000 iPhones in a 24-hour day, or more than 90 a minute, as of September 2010.[17] Management used stop-watches and computerized industrial engineering devices to test the capacity of the workers and if workers being tested were able to finish the quota, the target would be increased day by day until the capacity of the workers was maximized. Another group of workers at Kunshan factory commented, "We cannot stop work for a minute. We are even faster than machines." A young woman worker added:

> Wearing gloves would eat into efficiency, we have a huge workload every day and wearing gloves would influence efficiency. During really busy times, I don't even have time to go to the bathroom or eat.

Foxconn claimed that production workers who stand during work are given a ten-minute break every two hours, but many workers said that "there is no recess at all," especially when the shipment is tight. In some departments where workers nominally can take a break, they are not allowed to rest if they fail to meet the hourly production target. Working overtime through the night in the electroplating, stamp-pressing, metal-processing, paint-spraying, polishing, and surface-finishing units is the toughest, according to workers interviewed.

Buyers of Foxconn products – the world's marquee corporations, including Apple, HP, Intel, Nokia, etc. – want their computers and iPhones fast to meet global demand. The corporations pressure Foxconn to compete against each other on price, quality, and delivery. To fulfill the requirement of speedy production and shipment deadlines, Foxconn transfers the work pressure to the frontline workers. For example, Apple has been trying to get its iPhone 6 model out to the market without delay, while keeping up with the availability of iPhone 5 models. This drive for productivity and quality leads to constant pressure on Foxconn workers. The electronics parts and components are assembled quickly as they move up the 24-hour non-stop conveyor belts. Posters on the Foxconn workshop walls and between staircases read:

> Value efficiency every minute, every second.
> Achieve goals unless the sun no longer rises.
> The devil is in the details.

On an assembly line in the Shenzhen Longhua plant, a worker described her work in precise detail:

> I take a motherboard from the line, scan the logo, put it in an anti-static-electricity bag, stick a label, and place it on the line. Each of these tasks takes two seconds. In every ten seconds I finish five tasks.

Workers reported competing with each other to get the production bonus. In the workshops, a company job-evaluation system of Grades A, B, C, D, and Distinction was applied to prompt workers to do overtime work and not to take leave, otherwise the bonus would be deducted. Under these circumstances, the pressure becomes unbearable.

Each frontline worker specializes in one specific task and performs monotonous, repetitive motions at high speed. The rotating day and night shift system and extreme work intensity take away any feeling of freshness, accomplishment, or initiative toward work. In the production process, workers occupy the lowest position, even below the lifeless machinery. "Workers come second to and are worn out by the machines," was one worker's insightful summary of the worker–machine relationship. Others shared a sense of low self-worth: "I am just a speck of dust in the workshop." This is the "renewed" sense of self that arises after countless lectures from section leaders and production line leaders.

Losing control over the labor process, workers' awareness of their positions was painful: "Fate is not in your own hands but in your superior's." On Foxconn factory floors, conversation on the production line between assembly workers is forbidden. "You'll receive a warning letter for breaking the rule," a female worker from Foxconn's Shenzhen Guanlan plant said. Managers operated a policy of demerit points to drive workers to work harder. A 22-year-old worker explained:

> The policy is used to penalize workers for petty offences. You can lose points for having long nails, being late, yawning, eating, or sitting on the floor. There's a whole load of things. Just one point means losing my monthly bonus.

A long working day of enforced silence, apart from the noise of the machines, is the norm. On certain assembly lines, workers, however, said that control over work pace was much more relaxed because their senior managers would not be present at the workplace and hence their line leaders could be a little bit more lenient to them. In the middle of the night, the workers said,

Sometimes we could talk and laugh if we didn't affect the production; sometimes we might fall asleep and fall down on the ground. If we woke up immediately and continued working, nobody would scold us.

For those workers who could not endure the work pressure and isolation, they quit within a few months. In the survey conducted outside of Foxconn's Hangzhou factory, a woman worker who had just quit said, "It is such a cold environment on the shopfloor. It makes me feel depressed. If I continue to work at Foxconn, I may commit suicide too."

LONELINESS AND FRAGMENTED LIVES

Foxconn provides workers with "conveniences" like collective dormitories, canteens, services, and entertainment facilities in order to incorporate the entire living space in the factory management, serving the just-in-time global production strategy. To a large extent, workers' living space is merely an extension of the workshop, from the sphere of production to the sphere of daily reproduction. Food and drink, sleep, washing, and other aspects of workers' daily lives are scheduled just like the production lines, with the goal not to satisfy workers' needs as people but rather to reproduce workers' physical strength at the lowest cost and shortest time in order to satisfy the factory's production requirements. The feeling of alienation is multiplied when the production lines extended from workshop to dormitory space. There is no true rest even after getting off from work at Foxconn. Workers with different jobs and even night-shift and day-shift workers are mixed into the same dormitory. As a result, workers frequently disrupt the rest of others because of different working hours. In addition, random dormitory assignments often break up existing networks of social relations, hindering communication and interaction between workers. In this lonely space, workers often felt like they were losing control over their personal and social lives.

All the Foxconn production sites feature a combination of factories and dormitories, and its Shenzhen facilities have an astonishing 33 company dormitories with another 120 rented dormitories in the nearby community. The Foxconn Group has now tried to shift production workers from its higher cost, overcrowded Shenzhen site to other facilities. The dormitory labor regime remains unchanged. Most migrant workers live in the dormitories, but they do not have a normal life in their "home" – they are living with strangers, not allowed to cook, and not permitted to receive friends or families overnight. Whether the worker is single or married, he or she is assigned a bunk space for one person. The private space is virtually reduced to one's own bed behind a self-made curtain.

From the perspective of labor control, these factory-provided dormitories mean that production and labor reproduction activities take place in a self-contained, all-encompassing geographical locality. It facilitates flexible production by imposing overtime work, as the distinction between "home" and "work" is blurred. The lengthening of a work-day to 24 hours to meet the global production schedule means that the appropriation of labor surplus is absolute. Such a socio-spatial arrangement strengthens managerial domination, wherein control over labor is extended from the factory shop floor to the sphere of everyday life. The dormitory labor system is a cost-efficient solution for companies like Foxconn to ensure that workers spend their off-hours just preparing for another round of production. Thus, workers face a double pressure within and outside the factory, to the extent that workers are stripped of social living spaces.

Company policy clearly isolates workers, making it difficult to organize collective actions. Local and friendship networks are weakened or cut off. A worker acutely observed:

> Our batch of new hires totaled 120 persons. Most of us came from schools in Hubei; mine has 20 people. The company divided us into

five different groups for training. After training, I was assigned to an assembly line. My new friends, whom I met during the training, were all placed in different positions…I consider this arrangement to pre-empt workers from "making trouble."

As a result, interpersonal relations between workers are very weak, despite the fact that most are in their late teens or early twenties. Now we begin to understand why some workers have taken their lives.

Tian Yu is a 17-year-old survivor. On March 17, 2010, this carefree girl who once loved laughing and flowers jumped off the fourth floor of the Shenzhen Longhua factory worker dormitory. Compared with over a dozen other young lives that passed away, she was lucky; she lived. Yet in some ways she is less fortunate, because her young body remains paralyzed after many surgeries, and she will spend the rest of her life in a hospital bed or wheelchair.

Inside the "forbidden Foxconn city," Tian Yu experienced a similar kind of existence to all other production workers: go to work, return exhausted from overtime work, go to sleep, have no free time to them-selves, and no "extra" time for anything else. A typical work day begins at 8 a.m. and finishes at 8 p.m. On the product-parts inspection line, she was often reprimanded by her line leaders for poor quality, rejected parts, and "not working fast enough." Her seven roommates in the dormitory were all from other business groups; there was no one with whom to share the hardships at work. In her only 30 or so working days, she could not overcome the deep state of helplessness, but chose to end her life. She calmly recalled in the ward:

I entered Foxconn on February 8, 2010 and asked to go straight to work the next morning. In the enormous factory, I lost my way. Finally I arrived at the line – late for my first day of work…At the time I should receive my first month's wage, I didn't get my wage-card. I asked my line leader what went wrong. She simply told me to inquire in the Guanlan plant [an hour away by bus]. There, I asked one after another and still couldn't find a clue. I was like a ball being kicked around. No one tried to help.

Anger and frustration pent up. Instead of going to work early the next morning, Tian took desperate action.

In the wake of the multiple suicides, Foxconn dormitories throughout the country were all wire-grilled. The company installed 3,000,000 square meters of safety nets which were hung around outdoor stairways of dormitory buildings to prevent employees from jumping. Workers now live in a literal as well as metaphorical cage.

CONCLUSION

We may say that Foxconn represents a new development of monopoly capital, generating a gargantuan form of global factory regime that dominates the lives of the new generation of Chinese migrant workers and creates new forms of hardship and suffering to such an extent that these challenges could not have been overcome by the previous generation of migrant workers. The market dominance of the million-strong Foxconn corporation is facilitated through a deepening process of China's economic transformation at the national level as well as a deepening alliance between business and local states. The astonishing speed of capital expansion across geographic spaces was achieved through an alliance with the Chinese state, especially at the local level. In particular, local states compete to entice Foxconn to set up new factory compounds in their territories so as to boost GDP growth under their jurisdiction, to the extent that they ignore labor law enforcement and hence labor protections. Foxconn's growth was facilitated by the Chinese state in terms of providing massive land, infrastructural support, and supply of labor, resulting in a distinctive management model and a global factory regime, leading to worker grievances and feelings of desperation.

We highlight that Foxconn as a form of monopoly capital generates a global "race to the bottom" production strategy and repressive mode of management that weighs heavily on the rural migrant workers who form its workforce, depriving them of their hopes, their dreams, and their future. Within the walled cities of Foxconn, workers are struggling to improve their lives in the face of a factory discipline requiring that they meet ever higher productivity demands. When the Chinese government does not enforce labor law, employers like Foxconn feel free to ignore state restrictions on overtime to flexibly meet global just-in-time manufacturing and logistical imperatives. On the factory floor, work stress associated with the "scientific" production mode and inhumane management is intense. Alienation of labor and the lack of social support are common experiences. Young migrant workers in their late teens to mid-twenties, who have been placed in the "first-class" Foxconn factory-cum-dormitory environment, experienced severe loneliness, anxiety, and alienation. Suicide is merely the most extreme manifestation of the migrant work experience for hundreds of millions. Contradictions between capital and labor ultimately have cumulated at the point of production and daily reproduction, resulting in widespread labor grievances as well as struggles.

7 Radicalization and Collective Action of the New Chinese Working Class

This final chapter concerns the collective action and possible radicalization of the new working class. As a result of 30 years of reform, the repositioning of China as a "workshop of the world" in the age of globalization has provided the bedrock for nurturing a new Chinese working class. The structure of production and domination embedded in the dormitory labor regime of the "factory of the world" embodies a new laboring subject of resistance. In spite of the subsumption of class hegemonic discourse, class opposition from capital, institutional barriers from the state, and lack of support from society, this new laboring class is fighting for its own class formation through a variety of actions, defiance, and resistance in their daily lives in both their working and living spaces. Notwithstanding the neoliberal project in China and worldwide to dislocate the existence of class, the new generation of the working class realized its class experience from below, and is now increasingly conscious of, and participating in, various forms of collective action. Working to remake its class, rooted in its life world, spontaneous strikes by migrant workers in South China have been multiplying since the mid-1990s (see Chan 2001; Lee 2002, 2007; Thireau and Hua 2003; Leung and Pun 2009; Friedman 2014). Recent years have further seen increasing numbers of collective actions among migrant workers pursuing delayed wages, demanding compensation for injury or death, or pressurizing enterprises to increase wages and living allowances (Friedman and Lee 2010). These actions include litigation, such as suing subcontractors or companies (Chen and Xu

2012), as well as collective actions such as sit-ins, strikes, and even suicidal behaviors (Pun and Lu 2010a, 2010b). Workers have taken action to confront capital at the point of production in the workplace as well as challenging power at societal levels in the courtroom, on the street, or in front of government buildings.

This final chapter focuses on questions of collective action of migrant workers, who are now the major force of the new working class, which is trying to alter its fate through labor struggles in the new age of global capitalism. By looking at the collective actions of migrant workers in the electronics and construction industries as examples, we ask the following questions: First, what is the nature of labor actions and what are the mechanisms of mobilization of the collective actions? Second, how can the shop-floor industrial relationship, legal system, and other institutional arrangements shape such collective resistance? Third, could these collective actions be understood as class actions, especially when framed by a discourse of human and legal rights? What is the relationship between legal action (supposedly a realm of civil society) and collective resistance (supposedly an area of class conflict driven by production relations)? In short, how could workers nurture class consciousness through their participation in collective actions and, most importantly, how could they make sense of their struggle through a radicalization process?

LABOR ACTIVISM IN CHINA

It is now estimated that more than 270 million rural migrant workers are working in the urban and industrial areas of China, and the number is increasing year by year. In the context of capital accumulation in Third World countries, China is the global center of production, which contributes to the making and remaking of the new Chinese working class. With the pouring in of transnational capital and restructuring of private capital, class differentiation, class conflicts, and class polarization now explicitly exist in reform-era China (So 2003). Lacking cultural capital and institutional channels to voice their grievances, subordinated classes now mobilize mass protests to demonstrate their discontent and resist suppression. In the course of economic reforms, Deng Xiaoping and his followers have striven to legitimize governance by replacing class struggle approaches with law and related institutions as an arena to mediate conflict through the courts rather than in the streets (Gallagher 2006; Gallagher and Dong 2011). New legal provisions passed since 2008, tested by workers in the labor dispute arbitration committees and courts, and particularly worker victories, were said to contribute to raising worker consciousness of labor rights.

Official statistics revealed that between 1993 and 2005, the number of mass protests had risen nationwide from about 10,000 to 87,000 cases – a nearly 20 percent annual increase on average. Also, the number of participants in these protests had increased from 730,000 to more than 3 million, and 75 percent of these protests were initiated by workers and peasants (Leung and Pun 2009). It is observed that these protests have not only increased in number, but also in average size, social scope, and degree of organization. The upward trend continued from the first ten years of the 2000s, reflecting widespread incidences of rights violations as the private sector expanded. Labor cases skyrocketed to 693,465, involving more than 1.2 million laborers nationwide during the economic crisis of 2008. These were mainly disputes over wage and insurance payments, illegal layoffs, and inadequate compensation payments (see figure 7.1).

Following the economic recovery, newly accepted arbitration cases fell to 600,865 in 2010 and further to 589,244 in 2011. In recent years, governments at all levels have directed workers to resolve conflicts through workplace-based mediation and other informal means, hence reducing arbitration caseloads. In 2012, however, labor dispute cases rebounded (641,202), showing deep tensions in industrial relations,

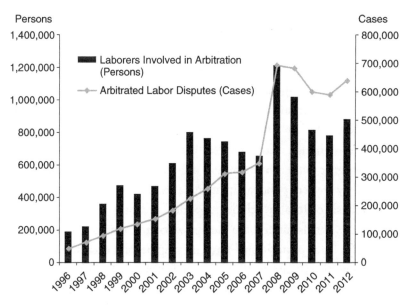

Figure 7.1: Arbitrated labor disputes in China, 1996–2012
Source: China Labor Statistical Yearbook 2013 (2014, table 9.1).

despite greater intervention than ever before from the government and its trade union offices.

Although systematic information on production days lost, arrested strike leaders, and picket-line injuries are not available in China, the statistics above reflect the widespread dissatisfaction and an increase in labor awareness among Chinese workers and peasants, in which the migrant working population in the Pearl River Delta (PRD) is a major actor. There is ample evidence that migrant workers are becoming more proactive in defending their rights, and they mobilize in actions of various forms, which include individual and collective action, especially direct action. This is to say, migrant workers' collective actions are not restricted to using established institutional or legal means to advance their interests. They are also undergoing a process of "radicalization," a process in which strikes, street actions, and demonstrations are often used.

The further polarization of class relations in China has also manifested in the current intensified labor conflicts and proliferating labor activism. Collective struggles such as demonstrations demanding pensions, road blockages by unpaid angry workers, and collective actions against illegal compensation are no longer exotic news for Chinese workers, whether in private, foreign, or state enterprises (Cai 2006; Chen 2007; Becker 2012; Butollo and ten Brink 2012). These collective actions, though mostly interest-based, are accompanied by a strong anti-foreign-capital sentiment and a discourse of workers' rights, and hence they are very political. In many cases, they are not only organized on the basis of locality, ethnicity, gender, and peer alliance in a single workplace, but also attempt to nurture workers' solidarity in the broader sense of a labor oppositional force moving beyond exclusive networks and strong ties (Fantasia 1988). Cross-factory strike tactics are sometimes used to invite workers from the same industrial region to participate in marches, street protests, or highway blockages.

LABOR ACTION OR CLASS ACTION?

Workers' resistance has developed from a single means to multiple means, from single-factory participation to cross-factory participation, from engaging only in legal actions to launching various collective actions (Pun et al. forthcoming). Usually workers targeted the factory management by demanding further state interventions as the state still claimed itself to be a socialist country working for prosperity and strength for its people. The language the workers learned in order to claim their rights is nevertheless provided by the central state through a discourse of legal labor rights. In order to alleviate the industrial tensions generated since the 1990s, the Chinese government issued a series of labor regulations and laws not purely to protect workers' labor rights but also to dissolve social conflicts between capital and labor. "Rule by law" thus becomes not only a slogan of contemporary Chinese society but also a means of political legitimacy for the Chinese party-state (Gallagher 2006; Lee 2007). It is also a process of de-politicization (de-ideologization) of the party-state, attempting to regain its political hegemony through a legal rationality. Hence an imagined "irrational" ideological society in the socialist period would be replaced by a "rational" legal society in the reform era, with "rule by law" used to defend a changing constellation of property rights and changing class relations. The belief in law is a political device that safeguards a changing political regime in the process of privatization and liberalization that contributes to a rapid transfer of wealth and reconfiguration of social class and status. Legalism is by no means created to support a civic participation culture, not to mention to protect workers' labor rights. And the workers have to learn this "truth" by their own actions.

Let us look at the collective actions of the construction workers we discussed in chapter 3. The political economy of the construction industry has shaped a specific labor use system – a labor subcontracting system. The system generates a specific capital–labor relationship in which the legal labor identity and labor relationship is highly subsumed. It creates a double absence in a legal sense: an "absent" boss and an "absent" labor relationship. This double absence led to a never-ending process of wage arrears and the struggle of the construction workers to pursue delayed wages in various ways, usually involving collective actions. Hence, the class relation was often subsumed and misplaced as a legal issue. What is interesting to us is that even though the issue of "double absence" surfaced as a legal problem, few cases of labor disputes that went through formal legal procedures actually reached the court. Instead, most of the labor disputes, after a series of labor actions, were settled through informal legal channels, especially through direct negotiations often involving violent struggles with the construction company.

With declining trust in the subcontracting system, conflicts arise on the construction sites as well as in the villages. Suffering the consequences of an unreasonable labor subcontracting system, the workers have learned that their labor rights are poorly protected. They do not usually take action until the fundamental basis of their consent – receiving wages at the end of the Lunar Year – is broken. When actions are taken, however, they are often of a violent nature, with fighting, bodily injuries, suicidal behavior, or attempts to damage buildings.

In January 2008 we visited Lan, a woman worker, in her dormitory on a construction site. Female workers account for only roughly 10 percent of the workforce on construction sites. She said:

> Young people don't understand hardship and tiredness. Our work requires working day and night. We wake up at four or five when the stars and the moon are still glittering and we work until dark comes. We only have very short breaks for meals. Even my pigs are fed better than me and yet I have to pay nine yuan a day for pig food.

The construction workers often talk about the hardship of their working life. Work hours in this industry are often irregular. A 13- or 14-hour work day is the norm, though the hours can be shorter in the winter. They refer to their jobs as bitter, dirty, and exhausting.

The main concern of the workers is the risk of industrial injury and death. However, a superstitious fear of mentioning the words injury and death means that they avoid discussing with their subcontractors the issue of compensation should the worst occur. One sudden death is illustrative. In March 2009, Pan, a 57-year-old worker from Hubei, had been working continuously on the site for three months without a day off and without pay. According to his two brothers who worked with him on the same site, he felt extremely ill when he returned from work to his dormitory one evening. The next day, Pan still could not get up to work, but had no money to go to the hospital. When his two brothers came to see him at 11:30 a.m., he was trembling and his face was grey. He died at 1:30 p.m., shortly after reaching the hospital. He had only 1.5 yuan in his pocket.

Pan's daughter came from Hubei to ask for compensation, but the subcontractor who had recruited her father had no money to do this. Accompanied by her two uncles and a nephew who worked in Beijing, she approached the labor-service company which had subcontracted the work. The company at first denied any labor relationship with her father, and then claimed that he had died of "natural causes," implying that this was not the result of an on-the-job ailment. The manager of the labor-service company finally told them, "Out of humane concern, we are willing to give you 20,000 yuan for the cost of a funeral." While the daughter hesitated about taking the money, an angry quarrel broke out between her nephew and the manager. The manager soon called in a dozen hired hands, who beat the nephew and threw them all out of the office. "Those men hit my head and twisted my neck. See my bruise, here." Infuriated, the nephew swore to take revenge, while the two uncles still hoped that the company could give them the money and their three-month wages so that the family could return home to arrange the burial as soon as possible.

Workers live on hope and despair. On a freezing winter's evening in 2008, we met Lan and her co-workers again in their dormitory on the construction site. The cold wind blew in through cracks in the walls. The below-zero temperature prevented them from sleeping in their exposed, unheated wooden hut. Work had been finished for a few days, but the workers' wages had not arrived, leaving them with an anxious wait before they could return to their hometowns. Lan and her co-workers were from a village in Hebei, and they were arguing with their subcontractor, who was trying to convince them to be more patient and to go on waiting for their payment. The argument was so loud that it attracted workers from other dormitories. Afterwards, Lan complained:

A group of Henan workers took action to fight for their wages yesterday. Why do we still have to wait? Wait for what? The Henan workers threatened to damage the villas that they built, and surrounded the office of the contractor on the construction site and didn't allow the office staff to leave. The staff then called the police and two police cars came. The manager of the company finally showed up and promised to pay the workers three days later...But how about us? We haven't managed to *nao* (make a noise and create a disturbance)! How could we get our wages!

Arguments and fighting were frequent on the construction site. The tense relationship between subcontractors and workers would often trigger violent acts that grew out of verbal disagreements. A number of times we observed severe fighting, either of groups of workers and their subcontractor, or of subcontractor and workers against their contractor. In December 2008, a subcontractor called up 20 of his workers to surround his contractor's office and demand payment. The contractor called upon his own hired hands, and a gang fight erupted in which a number of workers suffered injuries.

Lan's group had been told by their subcontractor that they would receive their wages on December 26. Some of her co-workers had already bought train tickets, hoping to return home immediately after receiving their three months' payment. On December 29 the subcontractor said that the company still had not paid him, and workers would have to wait until January 3. That day also came, but the workers still did not see their money. Anxiety and anger mounted.

On the evening of January 4 we visited Lan again. She anxiously asked for our help:

You are educated people. You know how to ask for our wages. Please let us know how to get our wages. We've toiled extremely hard for three months, and now we have no money to go back home. How can we support our family and our children?

One of her co-workers, Ting, jumped into our conversation and said,

> We have to *nao*. We have to show our muscle. When we were working, they [the quality controllers sent by the contractor] came to monitor and fuss about our job. Every day we were watched. But now that our work has finished, we are dumped. We are nobody. We have to *nao* to ask for our wages!

Both in the city and in the village, *nao*, creating a disturbance, was the word used most frequently when the workers talked about demanding their delayed wages. Despite the delays, some of the workers felt that *nao* was not an appropriate strategy, as it often involved breaking up relationships and disturbing social harmony. Driven by their experiences on the building site and by desperation, however, most of the workers found no other appropriate weapon to defend their basic labor rights.

The long wait for wages usually created despair and anger. Lan and her co-workers asked their subcontractor to provide a written guarantee that their wages would be paid in full within three days. It was often the case that when the boss finally had the money to pay the workers, the original pay rate would be cut by 20 to 30 percent. One Sichuan worker explained, "We were told we would have 70 yuan a day. Now they say they can only give us 50 yuan. Take it or leave it, it's up to you. Take it, and you can go home. If not, you can wait." Eventually he had to accept. The workers' bargaining power was minimal, once all their work was completed and they were eager to return home. Once the construction work was completed, workers lost the chance of interrupting the work process in order to demonstrate their power of solidarity. Staying on the construction site without work was like a punishment. They still had to pay for their meals and other daily expenses. Waiting in the city thus means a double loss: workers cannot return home in time to help with the harvest, and have to pay for daily living costs.

With little choice, Lan's co-workers insisted that they should take action to back up their wage request. Action was forced. Ting feared simply waiting: "What do we do if January 6 comes and the boss still has no money to pay us? We can't wait any more!" A heated discussion followed, until a consensus was reached: to visit the offices of the Construction Ministry the next day and ask the officials for help. While some of the workers prepared a petition letter, others collected information about their contractor and evidence of their labor relationship, while still others tried to find out the Ministry's address. The workers went without sleep that night to prepare for the visit to the Ministry office, a place completely strange to them and located in the central part of Beijing. Three workers, including Ting, were chosen as representatives to see the official. It is traditional that, when the weak need help, they request a meeting with officials in the government office.

The workers travelled for three hours by bus to reach the Ministry building. They arrived at noon, hungry and cold, to be told by office staff that they were in the wrong place. Because they did not have a labor contract, they had to go to the Labor Bureau for help. It took a further hour to reach the Labor Bureau, where they were told to go to the District Labor Bureau, because they could not bypass bureaucratic levels – they were required to ask for administrative help at the lowest level. In the late afternoon, the workers finally got to the district office, which was crowded with workers from other construction sites, all caught in the same impasse of wage arrears. Ting said,

> Some workers were squatting quietly in the corridor waiting to see the officials. Some, however, were very agitated and shouted that, if they still couldn't get their wages, they would climb up to the top of the building and jump off.

Workers from other groups applauded the suggestion and screamed loudly that only by attempting suicide would the boss listen to them and repay them on the spot. "No boss has a conscience" or "all bosses have the worst conscience" were the most frequent utterances.

Ting and his co-workers, though, were still at a point of seeking redress by appealing to the authorities. He and his co-workers waited for an hour and a half to get in the door of the legal aid department of the District Labor Bureau. The first question put to them was whether they had a labor contract. They were told that the Labor Department could not help them if they did not, as they did not have a legal employer. The officer, though polite, told Ting and his co-workers to go back to their dormitory, but promised to phone the contracting company the next day to try to resolve the situation.

The staff of both the Construction Ministry and the District Labor Bureau know that most workers in this industry are not automatically given a labor contract. Ting asked, "If a labor contract was that important, why doesn't the government enforce it seriously? Why do none of us have a contract?" He felt very angry at being sent from department to department.

When the three workers returned to their construction site in the late evening, they could not calm down and repeatedly declared that if their money did not come, they had no other choice but to fight: "It's not a normal industry! We workers have worked for no wage!…If they don't give us our money, I'll lay down my life to fight them. How can they dare not to give us our money?" That evening, however, Ting had not yet reached the point of pushing for actual violence. Instead, he started to mobilize the other workers to make a banner for a demonstration, that read: "Give back my money stained with my blood and sweat!" Such demonstrations are often the last step before physical conflict. These conflicts were not isolated cases; most of the workers we interviewed had participated in collective actions in one way or another.

The nature of the construction industry and the struggle upon the completion of construction work means that labor actions are taken outside the sphere of production and therefore did not provide a threat to the production process. Unlike factory work, once workers went on strike during the production cycle, the profits of the company would immediately be affected. Self-destructive acts or violent protests are thus often threatened when construction workers find no way out. In the same month of 2009, at another construction site that we visited, a worker climbed onto a bulldozer, threatening to commit suicide if his pay continued to be withheld. The construction company called the police, who ordered the worker to climb down but also asked the company to pay the delayed wage to him. In February 2014, a threat to commit suicide ended in death when the worker accidentally fell. Other workers have been known to take up axes and sledgehammers, surround the villas that they had built and damage the buildings. In June 2014, a group of construction workers surrounded and wrecked a sales office as it prepared to welcome customers in the morning. The workers yelled, "The company cares about customers, but not us!" This drew the attention of the property developer, who put pressure on the construction company to resolve the wage arrears. Blocking roads to attract the attention of top officials in the central government is also a popular method of resistance. Only by creating disturbances to city life have the city's builders been able to secure their wages.

Among the construction workers, collective actions are mostly centered on the issue of wage arrears and compensation for injuries stemming directly from the sphere of production, which determined the nature of the workers' actions as class actions. Suffering from an unreasonable labor subcontracting system, the construction workers gradually learned that their labor rights were hardly protected. In spite of the hegemonic discourses, which put emphasis on legalism in regard to the labor rights of Chinese migrant workers, few construction workers, however, attempt to take their legal action or even labor arbitration. Most workers directly launch individual or collective action, fighting against the construction companies or pressurizing the local government to protect them. The reason behind this, paradoxically, is also due to the "double absence" of the boss and the capital–labor relationship in a legal sense.

Remember the story of Lan and her co-workers, when they tried to argue for their delayed wages from their subcontractor, they said "You have to give us a sliver of justice or fairness, *gongdao*, working for no money is simply against the law of heaven," one worker said. "We trusted you and we relied on you to chase for our money: our money tinted with blood and sweat! Keeping our wage is against the law, *weifa!*" another worker added. During the argument with the subcontractor, the language the workers often used is *gongdao* (the principle of justice) and *weifa* (against the law).

Justice and law, however, embodied different meanings when the workers used these concepts. The term *gongdao* is a calling to morality derived from a basic belief in human fairness embedded in the order of heaven and the cosmos. In the eyes of construction workers, *gongdao* is more basic and fundamental once it is challenged. Hence fairness, with its belief rooted at the community level, is a habitus concept, while the concept of law, with its provisions given by the state, is a formal legal concept. Using these two concepts intermingled, we found that the workers made stronger claim by using *gongdao* (the principle of justice) than *weifa* (against the law), and they were more angry when fairness was transgressed.

Law is a new belief in Chinese society, created by the Chinese state as part of its neoliberal transformation in the reform period. As a new ideology, it actually occupied a supreme status in providing understanding of the normative behaviors of social agents, be they peasants, workers, or bosses. However, if "building a legalized society" is a progressive attempt in the eyes of the Chinese elites, it is less so for peasants and workers who understand their social lives by the principles of justice, humanity, and morality. "To ask for an explanation," often used when the construction workers went to the office of the construction company to demand their delayed payment, is to ask on the grounds of morality and justice, but not the rationale of legal practices.

Most of the time workers are very anxious to wait for their wage so they can return home for family reunion at Chinese New Year. The struggle at the construction site – simply to fight for their delayed wage – is often understood as a bottom-line struggle as it exposes the violent nature of the subcontracting system, which the workers do not have any difficulty in understanding as causing their exploitation. As the concept of class was seriously suppressed in the reform period, what substituted for it is the language of "fairness" or "justice" – a market discourse that imagines an equal opportunity for all given equal competition. A problem of "inequity" arises when this equal opportunity is thwarted.

As a mother of three children, Lan, the female construction worker, was less patient than the men to keep waiting for her delayed payment. She had been away from home for half a year to work on the construction site. The only reason for her to leave her children in the village was to earn money for her family. Working for no money was simply unacceptable! Taking actions to demand their money was morally legitimate, be they legal or illegal. Arguments and fighting were frequent phenomena on the construction site. The workers called for direct actions instead of legal means to resolve their labor disputes.

It is clear that the workers seldom used the word "class," but used the language of justice and law as a substitute. In brief, the principle of injustice refers to the unfair treatment of individuals by others who transgress the minimal requirement of moral standards of society at large. A discourse of "rightful resistance" seems to overshadow the discourse of "class action" in the way that the workers make sense of their suffering in terms of an embedded morality rather than class exploitation. To look deeper, however, we find that the accusation of the principle of injustice lies squarely at the core of the capital–labor relationship, i.e. the production relation of the construction industry which underwent a rapid change in the nature of capital and structure of the industry during the reform period. The political economy of the "no boss" and "no labor relationship," a delinking of capital and industry, and of management and labor, also hooks up directly with the specific and exploitative nature of the labor subcontracting system. All the labor struggles stemmed from this changing political economy of the construction industry which imbued them with a class nature.

WORKER STRIKES IN THE DORMITORY FACTORY REGIME

Let's turn from construction workers to factory workers in order to understand the development and mobilization of workers' collective actions and their claims under the dormitory factory regime. The rise of a new class of Chinese rural migrant workers, many of them in the service of domestic and transnational capital, has led to a wave of protests demanding labor rights and protections. Suicide or quitting are not the only worker responses to capital we have observed. Every year many more workers, looking for a better life, come to the city. They soon become disappointed, get angry or anxious, have grievances, and finally they turn to direct actions. When and how did migrant factory workers begin to take part in collective labor activism? What were their grievances? How did they understand their action in opposition to capital and state, and how did they develop class solidarity from their experience from below?

Remember the story of Xin in chapter 4. A deepening process of semi-proletarianization created under the dormitory labor regime was the setting in which we met Xin, a labor activist who had been working in a Shenzhen-based Disney supplier factory, H Toys, in February 2007. We encountered Xin and his co-workers during their prolonged pursuit of workers' rights by means of a series of collective actions.

Starting from that moment until 2008, Xin and his co-workers had no moment of peace and comfort, as they carried out a series of long-lasting battles against factory relocation and to secure fair compensation in the Shenzhen SEZ. As it turned out in the story of Xin's struggle, the management only wanted to retain the managerial and supervisory staff, as it convinced them to relocate to the new factory. The management also aimed to keep "loyal" workers who had been working with them for more than five years. This applied to only a few workers because the majority of the workforce was unwilling to leave the company without compensation and accept the 25 percent salary cut in the new factory. With less overtime work during the struggle, workers stayed in their dorms more and thus had more opportunities to discuss and work out strategies for receiving their overtime compensation. They read labor regulations issued by the Shenzhen government and discussed the laws among themselves. Some groups of workers started to collect reports of violations by the company and wrote them down. These violations involved payments, deposits, working hours, working conditions, contracts, and social security insurance. Within the close confines of the dormitory, the workers organized meetings in groups, created networks, and agitated to make it known that the company was operating illegally by being in breach of laws and statutes. Through this process of organizing workers inside the dormitory, the collective consciousness of the gaps between the company's practices and regulations was effectively nurtured. Militant collective action would be expected sooner or later. Hence, the dormitory labor regime, as anchored and connected places – or battlefield sites – open up a new possibility for class formation and labor organization that challenge the abstract space dominated by the state and global capital. Control and resistance are all squarely built into the architecture of the dormitory labor regime that nurtured daily and collective class struggles rooted in the migrant workers' class experiences from below.

By the time we met Xin, he and four of his co-workers had already left the factory. H Toys, a factory of 600 workers, was organized under the typical dormitory labor regime. While 80 percent of the workers stayed in the factory-provided dormitories, the remaining 20 percent lived in a nearby village where the rent was subsidized by the company. In February 2007, when Xin left, he was a skilled worker and foreman of a department specializing in crafting molds. Xin quit his job at H Toys after working there for one year so that he could take part in collective action against the company. He recalled that, when he left the factory for the last time, he found himself with no way forward and no way back. He was lost in the city where he had been working for ten years and where he had met with only a little success in his career. The plight of Chinese migrant workers is so commonly shared that even the workers we met in Shenzhen and Dongguan who had been employed in the cities for more than ten years still found it impossible to reside there. The longer they work in a big city, the more aware they become that they are excluded both socially and spatially. Rural migrant workers could sometimes stay in the city after a few years of working in a factory if they could become small storeowners, hawkers, or garbage collectors. However, they were still displaced and transient residents, with no hope of becoming proper citizens. This is a defining feature of China's urban political space that sustains an incomplete proletarianization commonly experienced by the first and second generations of migrant workers (Pun and Lu 2010a).

In early 2007, when Xin found that his factory had decided to relocate outside Shenzhen to reduce production costs, he mobilized his co-workers, who together embarked on a series of collective actions. Working within the disciplined and surveilled space, Xin and his workers nevertheless utilized the condensed dormitory space to hold meetings frequently in workers' dorms, turning the space into a subversive one. Xin recalled, after intensive discussions in their dorm rooms, all the 30 workers in the modeling department elected Xin and another four co-workers as workers' representatives to launch a lawsuit against the local labor bureau for failing to respond to workers' demands and for failing to implement administrative measures that would protect the laborers.[1] The five workers were later known as the "five gentlemen of labor-rights protection" and they became famous labor militants. Of the five workers, only Xin was from Henan. The other four hailed from other provinces, including Hunan and Jiangxi. All of these workers had belonged to the same production unit (the molding department) and had risen to the status of molding masters, and hence they were trusted by the ordinary workers even though heated debates were always held in their rooms. They were all in their thirties, and the oldest, Huang, had worked in the factory for five years and earned up to 4,200 yuan a month. Xin had only worked there for one year; he made around 2,200 yuan a month.

Conflicts with the management in the factory united the workers as militants, while staying together in the dormitory facilitated their organization and mobilization. At night, the five workers also listened to the radio, especially to programs on legal rights and work issues. Xin said that listening to the broadcasts was an "act of enlightenment": they learned that working without a contract was illegal and that overtime work should earn double or triple pay.

On February 12, 2007, the five workers launched industrial action, declaring that the factory was an illegal operation. They submitted a written notice of "collective revocation of labor relations" to the factory management, on the grounds that the management had failed to sign lawful labor contracts and to pay social insurance premiums, had forced them to work overtime, and had not paid overtime premiums on weekdays, weekends, and statutory holidays. At the same time, the protesting workers urged the district labor officials to defend workers' legitimate rights. Specifically, Xin and his colleagues demanded that the officials ensure that the factory would shorten its working hours to the legal limit, sign lawful labor contracts with employees, enroll in social insurance schemes, and pay wages and overtime premiums for January and February 2007. Most strikingly, the five workers demanded back pay for two years of overtime work; the back pay amounted to 650,000 RMB. They stated their points clearly:

> Employees are required to work at least 28 days a month and 13 hours a day. Overtime premiums were only paid when one worked for more than 9 hours. However, the illegal underpayment of the workers amounts to between 1 and 1.2 yuan per hour. There is no overtime premium at all for pieceworkers.
>
> Take the example of Huang XX: in December 2006, he worked 227 hours (considered a "normal" workload), plus 114.5 hours of overtime work. In January 2007, he worked for 266 hours, with 87.5 hours of overtime. Or Chen XX: in December 2006, he worked for 269.5 hours, plus 77.5 hours of overtime.

Still, the catalyst for the collective action was the factory relocation. Anger, frustration, and a sense of unfairness were mounting in the workplace. The fear of layoffs and the difficulty of acquiring overtime compensation after the factory's relocation reinforced the protesting workers' determination to take action. As one of the five, Huang, observed,

> We are among the few core skilled workers in the factory. I earn around 4,000 yuan every month; that's not nothing. I don't have to worry about what to eat or drink. But we lack a sense of security. We also don't have a decent self-image. Despite the dedication of our youth and sweat to Shenzhen, we've been displaced and are ultimately disposable. When we get old, contract chronic occupational diseases, and go home, what can we do without old-age pensions and health insurance?

Huang made it clear that he was not discontented with his working conditions or salary; what worried him was the future, the prospect of neither security nor dignity. As a replaceable laborer, he was aware of his vulnerable position. When he became old, he would be let go by the factory, would probably be suffering from a chronic occupational disease, and would – of necessity – return to his home town. It was this sense of no future and no dignity that precipitated his anger and grievances in his professional life.

The five workers felt that they had little choice but to take action. In their mid-thirties, they had all reached the limit of their career advancement, and what awaited them was inevitable decline and probable replacement by younger workers. They all knew that the skills they had accumulated could be learned by others eventually. Caught in the limbo of no reaction from the factory management, they had little choice but to take radical action. The target of their action shifted from the factory management to the local government. Eagerly acquiring information on the Internet, Xin and his co-workers soon figured out that the local labor bureau should be responsible for monitoring working conditions and handling labor disputes.

During the course of litigation by these five activists, 600 production workers of H Toys, most of whom were women, also organized a strike. In May 2007, the factory signed short-term contracts with its employees and announced that the factory would relocate the facility to Dongguan by the end of the year. By September, the women workers had united to stage collective work stoppages, protests, and revocations of their contracts. They demanded unpaid overtime premiums, financial compensation, and the social insurance they were owed (*Southern Metropolis Daily*, September 12, 2007). "No boss has a conscience" was the frequent refrain of the workers when they walked out the dormitory building with their luggage.

The sense of the disposability of labor was particularly strong at H Toys, not only among the women workers who resigned but also among those who chose to stay. The women workers were further aggravated when the management argued that, according to labor law, the company was required to give workers only 24 hours' notice of contract termination, and thus no compensation was needed. The one-month compensation offered should be considered a benefit, not a right. Workers should be content to leave, even though they had worked for the company for up to six years.

In July, the five workers took their case to court for the second time. They submitted a detailed account of the mishandling of their complaints by the labor bureau. They further demanded that the previous statement be overruled. More important, they insisted on economic compensation and the right to safeguard their interests: "We do not have hopes for winning over the government departments or for successfully claiming our compensation. But we do wish to create a new possibility – to point to a new path of safeguarding our rights that would be helpful to workers" (*Nandu Daily*, July 25, 2007).

Having waited for legal action for a year, three of the five workers – Xin, Huang, and Chen – finally took their case to Beijing in April 2008. It was their last chance to seek help from the central government: "Going to Beijing is the last step. We have taken almost every step we could. Now it is the last step, and we don't want to miss it," Huang said. During their five days in Beijing, they visited the Ministry of Labor and Social Security, the Petition Office of the People's Congress, the Supreme People's Court, the State Department, and ACFTU.[2] Their reception filled them with despair. Later, Xin and Chen claimed the trip to Beijing was worthwhile because, after being expelled by the Petition Office after hours of queuing, they realized that they were on their own: "I finally lost my confidence in the Party. I still had some hope before I went," Chen said. The politics of resentment was transformed into a sense of desperation and an acute understanding of the wretchedness and helplessness of working people: "We have to rely on ourselves. We can't trust the government; we can't trust the management. We simply want a speck of justice."

A RIOT IN FOXCONN

Foxconn workers were often remembered because of the suicide wave that happened in 2010. Their resistance and collective action were seldom recorded and studied. During our research on Foxconn workers in the past five years, stoppages, sit-ins, demonstrations and even riots in different Foxconn facilities occurred frequently.

A Letter to Foxconn CEO, Terry Gou

Following a riot that broke out on September 24, 2012, Yu Zhonghong, a 21-year-old high school graduate with two years of work at Foxconn Taiyuan, wrote an open letter to Foxconn CEO Terry Gou, the first such letter in Foxconn's history:

> If you don't wish to be again loudly woken at night from deep sleep,
> if you don't wish to constantly rush about by airplane again,
> if you don't wish to be investigated again by the American Fair Labor
> Association,
> if you don't wish your company to again be called by people a
> sweatshop
>
> Please use the last bit of a humanitarian eye to observe us.
> Please give us the last bit of human self esteem.
>
> Don't allow your hired ruffians to hunt for our bodies and belongings,
> don't allow your hired ruffians to harass female workers,
> don't let your lackeys take every worker for the enemy,
> don't, because of one little error, arbitrarily berate or, worse, beat
> workers.

Please be clear, the true cause of imminent destruction of your
    industrial empire
cannot be one or two errors in the manufacturing process,
cannot be one or two workers' suicide,
cannot be the theft of one or two computer mice or other official items.

Please be clear, the true cause of the imminent destruction of your
    industrial empire
is this strict hierarchical system,
it is this thing called privilege.

Beginning late at night on Sunday, September 23, 2012, and continuing through the morning of September 24, tens of thousands of workers rioted at the 80,000-worker Foxconn Taiyuan factory in Shanxi province, causing the shutdown of entire production lines for that day and disrupting the manufacturing of iPhone 5 metal parts. Several dozen workers were brutally beaten and seriously injured by company security officers when they came to support a group fighting at the workers' dormitory area, and 5,000 armed police were dispatched to the scene. Shanxi provincial governor Wang Jun also rushed to the plant to "restore law and order." This industrial action is worth noting not only because of the scale of protest, but also the workers' leaders were able to voice their condemnation of the whole production system of the industrial empire and they overtly made their demands. Yu Zhonghong and his co-workers courageously demanded of both the company and its union that they act responsibly toward the workers. The open letter to Foxconn CEO Terry Gou ends with three "remembers":

Please remember, from now on, to treat your subordinates as
    humans, and require them to treat their subordinates, and their
    subordinates, and their subordinates, as humans.

Please remember, from now on, to change your attitude that Taiwanese are superior, those of you who are riding a rocket of fast promotions and earning wages as high as heaven compared to those on earth.

Please remember, from now on, to reassign the responsibilities of the company union so that genuine trade unions can play their due role.

Yu Zhonghong, a member of the post-1990 generation growing up in the era of massive rural to urban labor migration, reflects on the shared experiences with his peers, the two hundred million rural migrant workers who have become the core of the new Chinese working class, yet find themselves acutely confronted with the class conflict of the dormitory labor regime. Many in this new cohort of migrant workers – second- and even third-generation youth who grew up living and working in the cities – are experiencing grievances and anger: "always yelled at," "self-respect trampled mercilessly," holding low-wage jobs, and at best, with slight chances to advance via education or training. If suicide is understood as an extreme form of labor protest chosen by some to expose an oppressive factory discipline in the industrial world, workers like Zhonghong and his co-workers are now standing up to defend their dignity and rights through direct class action. This is particularly telling at a time when China has begun its transit from a nation with a large labor surplus and a relatively youthful population, to one with tight labor markets and an aging population (Gu and Cai 2011), a situation that is driving wages higher and prompting corporations to transfer operations to lower wage areas in China's interior. Foxconn is no exception.

It is clear that the sense in which "right" is used in workers' strikes or riots is not narrowly confined to the realm of legal rights. For human dignity and the shared interests of workers living "at the lowest level" in Foxconn, Zhonghong angrily called for talks with CEO Terry Gou "on an equal footing." The sense of equity was embedded in the workers' worldview with a strong urge to ask for fair treatment. He also demanded the right to worker organization from senior management and requested a genuine company union be set up in order to protect the workers.

Looking back, at the Foxconn Taiyuan factory, labor discontent grew in a series of open conflicts from the beginning of 2012. A strike took place in March 2012 and six months later, factory-wide riots erupted on September 23–24, prompting Zhonghong to send the open letter. One of Zhonghong's co-workers recalled, "After the Spring Festival holidays, assembly-line workers received a wage increase of only tens of yuan to a maximum of one hundred per month, while our managers enjoyed increases of several hundred yuan and many more benefits. We're very angry about unfair wage policies." On payday (March 13, 2012), some 1,000 workers from Building A9 downed their tools to demand higher pay. They marched to the main factory gate chanting, "Strike! Strike!" They blocked the company entrance and the road for half an hour, disrupting traffic, and prompting the police and government officials from both the Xiaodian District and Taiyuan City to intervene. While Foxconn paid workers in accordance with the legal requirements over wages, the strikers demanded a pay raise above the legal minimum. In staging their collective actions in the street, they alarmed the stability-obsessed local authorities. The police force, supporting management, quickly broke up a 50-person picket line and pressured all the remaining workers to return to the factory and go back to work.

During the first half of 2012, Foxconn launched a huge recruitment campaign to gear up production at the Taiyuan plant. The brief strike did not win workers a wage rise. Grievances over wages and benefits, speed-ups, and humiliating treatment of workers remained unaddressed. Communication between workers and management, particularly top Taiwanese as well as Chinese leaders, was blocked. At about 11 p.m. on September 23, "a number of security officers severely beat two workers for failing to show their staff IDs. They kicked them until they fell to the ground," a worker said. A "bloody fight" between several security officers and workers at the male dormitory, and the screams of the victims, alerted many others in the darkness.

"We cursed the security officers and demanded that they stop. There were more than thirty of us so they ran away," a participating worker reported. But not for long. A squad of 50 security officers marched to the dormitory, infuriating the assembled workers. At midnight, tens of thousands of workers smashed security offices, production facilities, shuttle buses, motorbikes, cars, shops, and canteens in the dormitory and factory complex. Many others broke windows, demolished company fences, and pillaged factory supermarkets and convenience stores. Workers also overturned police cars and set them ablaze. The security chief used a patrol car public address system to order the workers to end their "illegal activities." The situation was getting out of control as more and more workers joined the rioting crowd.

Zhonghong explained, "The beatings by the security guards simply provided the spark. Over these past two months we couldn't even get paid leave when we were sick." The ever-tightening, shorter iPhone production cycle pressured workers and frontline managerial staff, so that workers could not even take one day off in a week, and the sick were compelled to continue to work.

While Foxconn was under pressure to fulfill targets for Apple and other brands, the potential for workers to display their power is great. Workers already understood that the best time to demonstrate their power and ask for improvement of working conditions is the time when management is rushing for the completion of production orders. Workers interrupted the continuous production flow by up to a day or two in an effort to force their employer and government officials, including the local trade union, to enter negotiations. This riot resulted in winning a wage increase and Foxconn eventually raised workers' wages to 1,800 yuan/month at its Taiyuan plant in 2013, 40 percent above the local minimum level. This was the beginning of the wave of protests whereby Foxconn workers were able to fight for their own rights collectively, sometimes violently, revealing the growing maturity of the new migrant working class.

RECENT TRADE UNION REFORMS

In the socialist period, especially during the Cultural Revolution, Chinese workers were encouraged not only to strike but also participate in factory management (Andreas 2008). Labor's right to strike was recognized in China's constitution in 1975 and 1978. At the time of reform and opening, in order to serve the opening for transnational capital, workers' right to strike was removed in 1982 and in subsequent constitutions. However, with the deepening of class conflicts and the maturity of the working class, neither this legislative change nor the legalistic hegemony prevented workers from going on strike. In times of crisis, workers have repeatedly taken multiple forms of collective action to secure their rights and interests. Labor and social unrest have been growing, fueled in part by a younger and better educated cohort of workers who are less tolerant of injustice and highly motivated to demand higher wages and better benefits.

Labor conflicts have become explosive in inland as well as in coastal industrial cities in recent years, and local governments have attempted to build grassroots or enterprise-level unions to become more responsive to worker grievances, among other interventions (Chan 2009). From the mid-1990s, against the background of radical restructuring that resulted in the loss of at least 17 million union members in the state sector between 1997 and 2000 (Traub-Merz and Ngok 2012), some government leaders have supported expansion of unions and greater worker participation in their activities. By December 2009, "unions had been set up in 92 percent of the Fortune 500 companies operating in China" (Liu 2011), including Foxconn, and this trend has continued since. As of January 2012, China had a total union membership of 258 million, by far the largest unionized workforce in the world (China Labor Statistical Yearbook 2013). Of these, 36 percent (94 million) were rural migrants, who comprised the fastest-growing segment of the unionized workforce since the early 2000s.[3]

Foxconn can be taken as an example to illustrate the effectiveness of this trade union reform in China. From 1988 through 2006, like many other enterprises, the company ignored its basic requirement under Chinese law to set up a trade union. It was only after a June 2006 report in a British newspaper exposing "iPod sweatshop" conditions in the Foxconn Longhua factory that produced the Apple iPod music player that the Chinese press took up issues of abusive treatment and illegally long working hours of workers. Foxconn countered by establishing a union at Longhua on the last day of 2006.[4] Ms Chen Peng, special assistant to Foxconn CEO Terry Gou, chaired the union from 2007 to the present.

The building of Foxconn's union in defending workers' rights and interests are illustrative of the experience of many Chinese workers. The Foxconn union organization mirrors the company hierarchy, from the assembly lines, business units, and business groups, to the corporate administrative level. At Shenzhen Longhua facility, as of August 2010, 249 union committee members were chosen from more than 400,000 workers. All union representatives are salaried Foxconn administrators appointed by management to union committees.

"Window dressing," commented the Foxconn workers on their trade union. "What is a trade union?" many young Foxconn workers asked us. A questionnaire survey of 1,736 workers conducted in the summer of 2010 revealed that the overwhelming majority, 92 percent of respondents, "do not understand the function of a trade union," which means that the workers did not understand what a trade union means (Pun et al. 2012). This is a paradox for the new generation of migrant workers, who were born and grew up in the post-Maoist reform period. Compared to their parents or the older generation of working migrants, this post-1980s generation – about two-thirds of the migrant labor force – has greater access to news and information, and has a greater expectation that their rights and interests will be protected. But they are lacking the basic knowledge of a trade union, and they do not even understand the function of a trade union because in their schooling, nobody has informed them.

The workers are encouraged to contact the trade union if they have grievances. And for those who do understand what a trade union is, they perceive the union as window dressing, merely organizing singing contests and box-sealing competitions. Li Xiaosheung, another 17-year-old migrant worker who seemed to know a little bit more about a trade union, stated:

> The [Shenzhen Longhua] trade union is merely a decoration. After the suicide wave, we were soon required to take part in the "Cherish My Life" rally. Since then, the union has organized smaller activities like day trips, singing and dancing performances, basketball tournaments, and partner matching parties on Valentine's Day. These could help workers relax to some extent.

The most frequent activities of the Foxconn union were the box-sealing competitions. Workers explained that "box-sealing is what happens after products are stuffed into boxes; the box is sealed. This is one operation on the production line. The competition is to see who can seal the boxes fastest." The thinly disguised productivity-raising game is framed as a team-building activity. "I'd say the union doesn't act according to workers' needs, but instead the activities are based on company needs," said Xiaosheung.

The absence of an effective union means workers' expectations remain very low. Mobilizing workers to join company events is burdensome. A staff member from the human resources department responsible for coordinating union activities, Miss Chen, explained:

There are a lot of different events. Every time it causes lots of trouble. Each department has to commit a certain number of workers to attend these events, say 1,000 or 2,000 persons. At the same time, the production line has to maintain the production target. We have to make announcements and bring workers to the events. We're tired of this.

At the Longhua and Guanlan facilities in Shenzhen, in 2011 the Foxconn union and the district-level trade union federation co-organized the Speech Contest. With monumental insensitivity, the theme was set as "I love the company, the company loves me." Liang and his co-workers "had no desire" to join the competition, even though the prizes were attractive. In other large complexes, Foxconn Kunshan (where the trade union was established in May 2007) and Foxconn Wuhan (where the union was set up in September 2011), similar activities and worker rallies were organized on the theme of "company love and care." Workers expressed that they preferred to spend their days off resting, rather than attending company ceremonies or chanting slogans.

In response to Foxconn employee suicides in 2010, dubbed the "suicide express" in local Chinese media, and under mounting social and political pressure, Foxconn proclaimed that workers would hold genuine elections for union representation and stated that its centralized union federation (of all factories across China) had expanded from four representatives in January 2007 to 23,000 representatives in December 2012, with membership reaching 93 percent of its million-worker-strong total workforce in China (Foxconn Technology Group 2014). A December 2013 Foxconn statement reiterated that "we have worked hard to enhance employee representation in the [union] leadership" and to raise employee awareness of the union's role in "promoting worker rights."[5] One year on, by the end of 2014, however, our study shows that Foxconn had disclosed neither specifics of a plan for democratic union elections nor specified the rights and responsibilities of worker representatives.

Despite the continued expansion of union membership, disputes over wages and job transfers have grown as the company accelerated its move to central and western regions, whose major cities are rapidly being transformed into mega production bases for global brands, including notably Apple, Microsoft, Samsung, and many others. The union has offered no response to the compulsory transfer of workers to lower wage regions. The institutional dependence of the Foxconn union on enterprise management and local government is a major obstacle to worker involvement or the protection of worker interests in workplace governance, grievance resolution, and collective bargaining.

The Chinese union institution is characterized by a dual dependence with state and capital working hand in hand (Chen 2009). In one of the world's largest "unionized" companies, Foxconn workers – like the more than 260 million rural migrant workers toiling in large and small workplaces throughout China – have no trustworthy communication channels through which to raise their voices, protect their rights, or collectively bargain. In the absence of an effective union and institutional support, workers in crisis have attempted to organize on their own, attempting various spontaneous forms rather than conventional trade union organizing. Association power is not limited to trade union organizing. It is unwise to state that Chinese migrant workers are lacking in associational power simply because of the absence of an effective trade union at the workplace. We witnessed workers' independent actions and their informal collective bargaining power organized through their own networks (Becker 2012). Spontaneous strikes through workers' informal networks seem to demonstrate more power rather than less.

CONCLUSION: THE GROWTH OF THE NEW GENERATION OF THE WORKING CLASS

Global capital and the reformist state have jointly turned China into the "workshop of the world" and Foxconn as the largest workshop. This is the backdrop of the world's workshop, and the new Chinese working class is now on the stage, experiencing their work and life, and beginning their life-long struggle. The emergence of the contemporary neoliberal form of global capitalism in China shapes the processes of industrialization and urbanization and hence structurally shapes the new working class which has no choice but to put up with it or resist it. Today, the global capital of accumulation, working together with the Chinese state, reproduces not only extended capitalist production of relations, but also multiple scales of contradictions, which open up new spaces for resistance by the new generation of workers.

Through looking into the collective actions of migrant workers in China, this final chapter sets out to make sense of the realities and complexities of the making of a new class. It argues that most of the recent collective actions involve workers' conflicts with management at the point of production, while simultaneously entailing labor organizing in workers' dormitories. Very often, these workers' actions poured into the streets or highways or workers surrounded the corporation's main office buildings, blocked company entrances, or local government buildings. They attracted media attention but also police repression. These labor actions are both economic and political in nature, as these direct actions immediately challenge the despotism of capital and the state apparatus.

In the face of the strong alliance of Chinese and international capital and the local state, aggrieved Chinese laborers have faced formidable obstacles to forming powerful organizations to sustain their fight for worker rights. Nevertheless, we have recorded their repeated wildcat strikes and escalated scale of struggles in the dormitory labor regime in the face of harsh repression. As we said before, the formation of the dormitory labor regime is central to the reproduction of China as factory to the world and the rise of a new working class. The entire ethic of the dormitory system was not just to impose severe discipline and punishment, but also to create a discourse on self-discipline, which was often emphasized at the workplace. This dormitory labor regime exemplified what Foucault (1977) described as internalized surveillance, deploying a series of disciplinary rules as well as subtle surveillance and meticulous self-supervision of everyday lives. In short, creating a well-trained workforce with discipline, directed to the maximization of production, is what we call "the political technology" of the dormitory labor system. This is exactly the place where the new working class was dissected, condensed, and displaced – a micro space of labor struggle embedded in a hegemonic project of subsuming class in the society at large.

However, the Foucauldian techniques of power over life in the dormitory did not really mean that a disciplinized workforce could be created. In contrast to the hegemonic project that attempted to announce the death of class in China, the workers fought against all discursive and structural constraints on them, namely neoliberalism, race-to-the-bottom global production strategies, the state's socialist *hukou* system, and the ambiguous peasant-worker identity, in the dormitory labor regime. None of the production workers really committed to workplace and dormitory rules. Instead of reliance on state protection to face a globalizing industrial world, the new *dagong* subjects have to actively manipulate their dormitory space for their own use. Overcrowding and intensive human interactions might cause conflicts among workers, but being together and sharing a "common fate" also weave and tie their working lives closely together. In everyday life, the migrant workers cluster along local, kin, and ethnic lines in the dormitories. They often depend on the support of local and familial networks they form. These networks facilitate migration flows, job searching, and the circulation of work information as well as help for the workers to cope with factory life and hardships in the city. Although these familial and ethnic networks benefit industrial capital in terms of recruitment, training, and discipline, they also provide the foundation for workers' bonds that help them to cope with an alien world. Reliance on these labor networks to train their workers, upgrade skills, and speed up the process of accommodation to factory life, means that workers learn about their own collective force, not only along lines of kinship, ethnicity, and gender, but also class (Pun 2007).

In times of crisis or strikes, the workers easily turn these "soft" supports from their local networks, ethnic enclaves, and collectives into hard resources for industrial struggle within their dormitories. In a number of the cases we collected, petition letters were circulated from dorm to dorm with signatures easily collected in a single night. Strategies against the management in times of wage arrears, bodily punishments, insults, or layoffs were discussed intensively among the groups and networks that had been formed in the micro space of dormitories. Participation in common causes against management could easily be organized through the dorms, as there was no space for dissenters from the "common struggle." Workers were efficiently organized and they spontaneously participated in strikes without any formal organizational help from trade unions or labor organizations.

Getting the workers' consent for the dormitory labor regime was always going to be problematic and it kept changing from the first generation to the second generation of the peasant-workers. Compression of the time needed for production in the dormitory labor regime works in favor of compression of the time needed for worker organization, thus shortening the time needed to generate workers' consensus and forming strategies for collective actions. To fight against the process of objectification, the workers had no choice but to defend themselves against being perceived as merely an abstract form of labor by actualizing their own value in their life-worlds. The "homing" of workers' life-worlds lies in the workers' dormitories – the new worker-subjects provisionally shelter themselves in the workers' dormitories provided by their employers. Here we encountered a local struggle where the dormitory not only served as a battlefield for fighting against capital, but also as a space of contestation for articulating a new class consciousness, and hence the making of the new working class of its own, despite the hegemonic power of capital and the state that works against its formation.

Moreover, we have observed a quick learning process among young migrants regarding organizing strategies, with the innovative and courageous actions of one group of workers leading another group to take similar actions, often within months in the same industrial area. Likewise, in the 400,000-strong Shenzhen Longhua facility, where, in the words of one interviewed production manager, labor conflicts and mini-scale strikes on "any calendar day" were virtually "uncountable," workers were acquiring organizing skills and raising their consciousness about the need for joint struggle to achieve basic rights. Rong Fang, a young woman from Hunan working in Shenzhen, is illuminating about the process of growing consciousness and solidarity among migrant workers in the course of struggles to redress common grievances:

> I didn't know that it was a strike. One day my co-workers stopped work, ran out of the workshop and assembled on the grounds. I followed them. They had disputes over the under-reporting of overtime hours and the resulting underpayment of overtime wages. After half a day, the central human resources managers agreed to verify the conditions. At night, in the dormitory, our "big sister" explained to me that I had participated in a strike!

In the factory-cum-dormitory setting, labor awareness among the youngest or newest groups of workers was raised. Fang and many other Foxconn migrant workers, many of them 16 or 17 years old, talked about their first involvement in collective labor protests. If the language of strikes and their participation is brand new to some workers, it is not new to others. High mobility of labor has facilitated the sharing of experiences of collective protests and strikes among workers. This is the bedrock for nurturing class consciousness of the new generation of the migrant working class.

However, the structural weakness of workers vis-à-vis management is also clear: the Chinese state has severely restricted collective labor rights, namely the right to organize and to strike, while local governments eagerly bid to secure production that will assure jobs. Nevertheless, in both the workplace and in the marketplace, migrant workers do possess structural and bargaining power. To date, this has been exercised primarily through wildcat strikes and riots, bypassing the official unions that serve the interests of management and the local state. With workers sensitive to opportunities presented by the demand by brands, such as Apple and other giants, to meet quotas for new models, they have repeatedly come together at the dormitory, workshop, or factory level to voice demands in timely ways. They are also quick to leverage the imminent labor shortage to boost wages, and have even scored a number of victories.

Although the development of an organized class movement is being restricted, factory-level strikes, work stoppages, collective bargaining on wages and social security, launching collective complaints, or actions like resorting to media exposure or the state apparatus are common means used by migrant workers to express their dissatisfaction and to ask for changes (Qiu 2009). The struggle at the construction site – simply to fight for their delayed wages – can be understood as a "bottom-line" struggle as it exposes the violent nature of the subcontracting system and the failure of the politico-legal regime to protect the basic labor rights of the migrant workers. The construction workers do not have difficulty in understanding the exploitative nature of the labor subcontracting system as it often causes wage arrears and bodily injuries without compensation. The struggle against "no boss" and hence "no labor relationship" is not a legal issue to them but a disguised class issue under the cover of a legal discourse.

The collective actions involved in this rapidly changing society induce angry, largely violent actions, sometimes a mixture of legal and illegal actions among migrant workers. The actions taken by the workers would usually surface as the fight for legal labor rights as the violations of their basic rights were legally sanctioned. However, this does not mean that the hegemonic discourse of "a legalized society" or legalism was successfully indoctrinated into the minds of the Chinese workers. Instead, the belief in legalism acts as a double-edged sword once the workers discovered that the law was not on their side. It collapses. Furthermore, the workers would learn that not only are their basic labor rights not protected by law but that they were actually excluded by it. This realization of the "uselessness" of legal weapons further agitated large-scale strikes or cross-factory protests.

According to E. P. Thompson, "class happens when some men, as a result of common experiences (inherited or shared), feel and articulate the identity of their interests as between themselves, and as against other men whose interests are different from (and opposed to) theirs" (Thompson 1966). In China's new industrial zones the language of class is subsumed and collective actions still lack a formal political agenda working against the capital-state nexus, but this does not mean that "interest-based" or "class-oriented" collective actions cannot germinate into political actions in this rapidly shifting society in the long run. Based on the organizational skills and collective awareness they acquired in the 1990s, the new generation of Chinese workers realized that in order to resist capital exploitation, they had to rely on themselves rather than legal stipulations or state support. We have observed the sense of self, the anger, and the collective action of the second generation of peasant-workers, and we have noted that these workers exist squarely at the center of a grid of controls and domination, where workers themselves have to negotiate and articulate their own agency. Despite the structural barriers, the new working class conjures up an array of everyday and collective forms of insurgency, which threatens the forces of capital, and makes the state ever more anxious to subdue them. Class opposition serves to reinforce collective identity, and vice versa. Through collective actions, the migrant workers were no longer atomized workers of a single workshop or production team. They developed a shared identity and consciousness from their daily experiences when they were taking part in action. As Gordon Marshall put it, "consciousness is, in fact, an integral component of social action ... [they] cannot be studied in isolation" (1983: 263). Consciousness is grounded in social action and the two must not be detached from each other.

The sheer reality of capitalist exploitation and state repression has transformed workers' class consciousness. This identification of a higher level of class interests does not mean that internal divisions such as work position, urban status, gender, locality, and others will immediately disappear. Such divisions do exist, creating internal dynamics in their organizing. In spite of the internal divisions, on the whole the construction workers or factory workers were able to build cross-site alliances and fight for their rights under unfavorable structural conditions. This potential unity was grounded by structural factors, as the Chinese workers were increasingly organized into the global production within the workshop of the world. In globalized China, private firms and transnational corporations, which supply global brands, transfer direct pressure to frontline workers and staff. At key nodes of global production and during peak seasons, a critical mass of workers acting together is capable of disrupting the continuous work flow, if only temporarily. In numerous ways, workers of different origins, gender, and work status are taking autonomous actions to defend their common rights and interests. These include the fundamental demand for meaningful union participation, but most often involve the pursuit of specific demands such as higher wages, benefits, social security, and safer working conditions.

At a time when the labor movement is on the defensive worldwide in an era of neoliberalism, economic crisis, and "austerity," an increasing number of spontaneous protests and direct actions by workers have taken place in China. These struggles foretell a gradual formation of a new Chinese working class in the age of global capitalism. In transnational production, the deepened class conflicts are fueling labor insurgency in the country. If the new generation of migrant workers succeeds in building their unions and autonomous worker organizations such as labor NGOs, their struggles will shape the future of labor and democracy not only in China but throughout the world.

Notes

1 China and Its Labor in the Neoliberal World

1 General Administration of Customs of the People's Republic of China, November 8, 2014. See http://www.customs.gov.cn/publish/portal0/tab49667/info691897.htm http://www.customs.gov.cn/publish/portal0/tab49667/info721618.htm.

2 Ibid.

3 Ian Robinson (2010) argued that taking into consideration the depreciation of the peso and appreciation of yuan, labor costs in Mexico are not as much higher as those in China as many people think.

4 World Bank, http://data.worldbank.org/indicator/NY.GDP.PCAP.CD.

5 http://www.aflcio.org/Press-Room/Press-Releases/AFL-CIO-s-Industrial-Union-Council-Joins-Fair-Curr.

6 *The World is Flat* was for some time a bestseller in China. Author Thomas Friedman advocated economic globalization and free trade and doing away with trade barriers between democratic nations to create an idealized leveled-out world where capital could flow freely on a global scale.

7 A phrase that was to become an important neoliberal slogan.

8 The University of Chicago was the major center for neoliberal ideology. As early as the 1950s the university sought to recruit students from Latin America who could be indoctrinated to become neoliberal economists. On their return to Latin America, these "Chicago elites" had a major influence on the continent's development model and were key promoters of neoliberal doctrine.

9 The *hukou* system requires every Chinese citizen to be recorded with the registration authority at birth, and have his or her residential categorization (either urban or rural) fixed. Citizenship benefits are tied to one's *hukou*. Only through government authorization can the *hukou* be changed.

10 Xinhua News Agency, June 8, 2014. Accessed at: http://news.xinhuanet.com/politics/2014-06/08/c_1111035497.htm (in Chinese).

2 Capital Meets State: Re-emergence of the Labor Market and Changing Labor Relations

1 "Liangshi shengchan 60nian bianqian" [Sixty years of change in grain production], *Liaowang Zhoukan* [*Outlook Weekly*], August 13, 2009.

2 See Guo Shutian, "Nongcun gaige 30 nian, zhuoli gaibian chengxiang eryuan jiegou – jinian Zhongguo nongcun tizhi gaige 30 zhounian" [Thirty years of rural reform, working to change the bifurcated structure of urban-rural relations – written on the occasion of the thirtieth anniversary of the institutional reforms in the Chinese countryside], in *Nongmin Ribao* [*Farmers' Daily*], November 21, 2008.

3 China Economic Net: intl.ce.cn/zgysj/200907/28/t20090728_19648885.shtml. See also Yan Hairong and Chen Yiyuan (2013) "From bean crisis to look at food sovereignty," *Nanfangchuan*, 19, 36–40.

4 The term "productive land" [*shengchan tian*] is based on a productive function perspective, where land is the major means of production for peasants. "Welfare land" [*fuli tian*], by contrast, is a term based on the perspective of the reproduction of labor, with land the basic source of means of subsistence.

5 In the era of the collective economy China established a system of social security and welfare provisions in the countryside, albeit below the level available to urban dwellers in either scale or quality. The main planks of this policy included the "five guaranteed households" – persons such as widows and the disabled who received welfare support – and subsidized grain. The costs of rural basic education were also met by the collective and in some more economically developed areas there were also other welfare measures. The basis for this social security provision was the state and the rural collectives.

6 See National Bureau of Statistics of the People's Republic of China, accessed at: http://www.stats.gov.cn:82/tjsj/zxfb/201405/t20140512_551585.html.

7 "'Wage' for 'Heart,'" CCTV News 1+1, June 7, 2010 (narrative in Mandarin).

8 ACFTU (All-China Federation of Trade Unions). 2011. "Survey Into and Some Proposals Regarding the Conditions of the New Generation of Rural Migrant Workers at Enterprises in 2010" (in Chinese).

9 On the discussion of Chinese citizens' right to pension insurance and their lack of access to workplace-provided social security despite legal requirements, see Mark W. Frazier, 2011, "Social Policy and Public Opinion in an Age of Insecurity," in Sarosh Kuruvilla, Ching Kwan Lee, and Mary E. Gallagher, eds., *From Iron Rice Bowl to Informalization*, Ithaca, NY: Cornell University Press, pp. 61–79.

10 Shenzhen implemented housing welfare reforms at all enterprises, regardless of ownership, starting in December 2010. The goal was to attract workers

from all over the country and to accelerate urban-rural integration. Both employers and employees – including Shenzhen permanent residents and migrant workers – are required to contribute monthly to the housing provident fund in accordance with municipal housing fund regulations.

11 International Monetary Fund (IMF). 2011. "List of Countries by Gross Domestic Product (Nominal) Per Capita, 2007." http://www.nationmaster .com/encyclopedia/List-of-countries-by-GDP-%28nominal%29-per -capita#cite_note-0.

12 The IMF list of countries at the low end of the per capita income spectrum also includes Laos, Burma, Kampuchea, and Timor-Leste, among others.

13 The Chinese government calculates the minimum wage using the concept of Engel's coefficient, based on the theory that the proportion of household expenditures on food declines as income rises. Engel's coefficient is used as a reference point to determine the subsistence needs of the poorest households. The 2004 Provisions on Minimum Wage Requirements refer to a household size of 1.87 dependents per income earner, and the Engel's coefficient of 0.604, which implies that 60.4 percent of income is spent on food.

14 *Xinhua*, February 8, 2012. "China Releases Plan to Create 45 Million Jobs."

15 China's National Bureau of Statistics (Rural Division). 2010. "Monitoring and Investigation Report on the Rural Migrant Workers in 2009." (in Chinese).

16 In 2010, there were 60,000 "super rich" Chinese with 100 million yuan (US$15 million), up 9 percent on the previous year. GroupM Knowledge – Hurun Wealth Report 2011. April 12, 2011. "Leading Authority on China's Wealthy Counts 960,000 'Millionaires,' up 9.7 percent, with Beijing Home to Most." "Billionaires," *Forbes*, March 7, 2012. See http://www.forbes.com/ sites/russellflannery/2014/03/03/2014-forbes-billionaires-list-growing -chinas-10-richest/.

3 Building China: Struggle of Construction Workers

1 In China, the construction industry is defined as the sector that creates buildings and other structures. See Han and Ofori (2001).

2 See National Bureau of Statistics, 2014 National Survey on Migrant Labor. http://www.stats.gov.cn/tjsj/zxfb/201504/t20150429_797821.html

3 See *Zhongguo jianzhu nianjian, 2008* (Statistics of China's Construction 2008). Beijing: Guojia Tongji Chubanshe, 2009.

4 See Report on China's Construction and Building Materials Industry.

5 Their work intensity, work hours, and payment methods are exploitative, but the rates of pay for construction workers are not as bad as those for workers in the manufacturing or service sectors.

6 See the report on *Xin Zhongguo jianzhu ye wushi nian* (The Fifty Years of New China's Construction Industry), published by a study group formed by the Construction Ministry (Beijing: Zhongguo Sanxia Chubanshe, 2000), p. 3.

7 See also Gail Hershatter's discussion of the use of the apprenticeship system in Tianjin in the early twentieth century, in *The Workers of Tianjin*, pp. 101–4.

8 See *Xin Zhongguo jianzhu ye wushi nian*, p. 6.

9 This was the "Tentative Provisions for Construction Industry and Capital Investment Administration System Reform." See *Xin Zhongguo jianzhu ye wushi nian*, pp. 7–8.

10 See the Construction Ministry's report on *Xin Zhongguo jianzhu ye wushi nian*, p. 8.

11 In August 1995, the State Planning Commission, the Ministry of Power Industry, and the Ministry of Transport jointly issued "The Circular on Granting Concession to Foreign Financed Capital Projects." The Construction Law was put into effect on March 1, 1998, covering a wide range of issues such as qualifications for entry into the construction industry, procurement and delivery of works, construction supervision, construction safety, construction quality, legal liability, market regulations, and procedures in construction projects.

12 The number of peasant-workers in the industry is listed in a 2004 ACFTU report, "A Survey on the Situation of Construction Peasant-Workers." See http://finance.sina.com.cn/g/20041111/17381148918.shtml.

13 The China Construction Bank is the major bank providing credit to large-scale construction projects, but only a small proportion of large enterprises have access to its services. Debt is said to be "triangular" when it involves a chain of debtors. See Lu and Fox (2001), pp. 13–15.

14 Villas are more complicated to construct than a high-rise building, so the subcontractors have to set aside more labor days for the completion of the work.

15 In the construction industry, workers used *gongqian* to describe their wages, but workers in the manufacturing and service sectors usually used *gongzi* (salary), a more formal concept.

16 The situation is like that for coal miners, who are at risk of serious injury or fatality because of frequent explosions in the mines, but who work there principally because of the relatively high rate of pay.

17 Strictly speaking, according to the Company Law and the Construction Law, the labor supplier subcontractors do not have corporate status, and hence do not have the legal status to employ workers.

4 Making and Unmaking of the New Chinese Working Class

1 *Time*, 16 December 2009, "Runners up: the Chinese worker."

2 See SACOM's statement, "Remembrance of the deaths of Foxconn Workers, June 8, 2010" at www. sacom.hk.

3 Andrew Ross asked a question, "Are the Chinese losing China?" in his book, *Low Pay High Profile: The Global Push for Fair Labor*. New York: The New Press, 2004.

4 See Stuart R. Schram, *The Political Thought of Mao Tse Tung* (New York: Frederick A. Praeger, 1969), pp. 236–7.

5 The process of proletarianization also refers to a process of turning non-wage labor into wage labor. As a result, the workers' fate depends on labor markets. They do not possess the tools they use, the raw materials they process, or the products they produce.

6 For example, the making of the English working class in the nineteenth century, the experiences of the "Four Tigers" of East Asian countries in the twentieth century, or the transformative experiences of South Asian and Latin American countries today. All these countries underwent a rapid rural-to-urban transformation, which relied on a working class that migrates from rural areas to settle in urban communities. Everywhere we can find examples of rural migrant workers streaming from countryside to work in industrial cities. These rural workers were allowed to stay in the city where they established family homes and larger communities.

7 This living experience is strikingly different from that of the urban middle class, which assumes that industrialization goes hand in hand with urbanization. Obviously, there is rapid urbanization in today's China, but this process is mainly driven by urban property capital. Industrial capital only plays a role in turning China into the world's factory.

8 As Richard Sennett and Jonathan Cobb put it, the hidden injury of class is the creation of a feeling of inadequacy embedded in the self through day-to-day life experiences. The self is induced to feel responsible for the inner anxiety arising from a sense of inadequacy or incompletion even though, in a society with a class structure, individuals are deprived of the freedom to control their life (1972: 36–7).

9 See the full story in Chapter 6 of *Made in China: Women Factory Workers in a Global Workplace*.

10 For the younger generation in rural China today, entering university is one of the only ways to leave the country and settle in the city with legal rights and potential economic support. Except for a few elites, the majority of the *nongming gong*, despite their position in the industrial hierarchy, cannot reside in the city on an equal footing with their urban counterparts. Among 1,455

workers we studied in Shenzhen and Dongguan, about 75 percent received junior secondary education. For the female workers, they often had less chance of getting into higher secondary schooling, not to mention entering a university.

5 Spatial Politics: Production and Social Production of the Dormitory Labor Regime

1 I owe much to Chris Smith who introduced me to the concept of the dormitory labor regime and who alerted me to similar labor practices in Japan, Korea, Latin America, and South Africa.

2 In Socialist China, the enterprise institution known as *danwei*, or unit, also provided workers with lifelong accommodation. As regards workers' welfare, *danwei* did not prolong the working hours of the workers.

6 Monopoly Capital in China: The Foxconn Experience and Chinese Workers

1 See SACOM's report on Workers as Machines: Military Management in Foxconn, October 13, 2010; Foxconn and Apple Fail to Fulfill Promises: Predicaments of Workers after the Suicides, May 6, 2011. See http://www.sacom.hk.

2 This chapter draws on material and findings from the collective efforts of Foxconn Research Group, an independent team composed of teachers and students from Mainland China, Hong Kong, and Taiwan to understand the Foxconn experience and its impact on young migrant working lives. Surveys and ethnographic studies were conducted off-site in major Foxconn factory areas in 11 cities: Shenzhen, Wuhan, Kunshan, Shanghai, Hangzhou, Nanjing, Tianjin, Langfang, Taiyuan, Chengdu, and Chongqing between 2010 and 2012.

3 Foxconn Technology Group. 2010. Global distribution. http://www.foxconn.com.cn/GlobalDistribution.html (in Chinese).

4 Foxconn Technology Group. 2011. "2010 CSER (Corporate Social and Environmental Responsibility) Annual Report."

5 Foxconn Technology Group. 2009. Corporate social and environmental responsibility report 2008.

6 Foxconn Technology Group. 2009. Corporate social and environmental responsibility report 2008.

7 Foxconn Technology Group (2010: 5; 2011: 4; 2012: 3; 2013: 4, 12; 2014: 3); Fortune Global 500 (2010–2014).

8 Quoted in "iPhone supply chain highlights rising costs in China," *New York Times*, July 6, 2010.

9 "Foxconn rides partnership with Apple to take 50 percent of EMS [electronic manufacturing services] market in 2011," *iSuppli*, July 27, 2010.

10 "A look inside Foxconn – where iPhones are made: a postmodern Chinese industrial empire that was blighted by suicides," *Bloomberg Businessweek*, December 9, 2010.

11 Foxconn Technology Group owns manufacturing facilities and research and development centers in Taiwan, China, Japan, South Korea, Australia, New Zealand, the Middle East, Southeast and South Asia, Russia, Europe, and the Americas.

12 Foxconn manages chain stores (e.g., *Wan Ma Ben Teng*, Media Mart [*Wan De Cheng*], and CyberMart [*Saibo Shuma Guangchang*]) in big cities, tapping into the growing domestic consumption markets. China's domestic market is expected to grow close to 10 percent in 2011, much faster than in either the United States or Europe.

13 See Total Population by Urban and Rural Residence and Birth Rate, Death Rate, Natural Growth Rate by Region, *China Statistical Yearbook 2014*, http://www.stats.gov.cn/tjsj/ndsj/2014/indexeh.htm.

14 Quoted in China.org.cn, October 28, 2010. http://www.china.org.cn/opinion/2010-10/28/content_21221326.htm

15 Quoted in "Chengdu factory's iPad capacity to reach 100 million units in 2013," *Chengdu Weekly*, January 2, 2011.

16 See Employment and Wage, China Statistical Yearbook 2010. http://www.stats.gov.cn/tjsj/ndsj/2010/indexeh.htm

17 "A look inside Foxconn – where iPhones are made: a postmodern Chinese industrial empire that was blighted by suicides," *Bloomberg Businessweek*, December 9, 2010.

7 Radicalization and Collective Action of the New Chinese Working Class

1 At the beginning of the collective action, a legal action rather than a strike was anticipated because the workers in the modeling department did not have enough confidence to organize a factory-wide strike. However, the action developed gradually into a strike during the course of the movement.

2 All-China Federation of Trade Unions is a state-controlled union, thus the only legitimate trade union in China.

3 This stands in sharp contrast to the United States, the United Kingdom, Australia, and many other countries, where private-sector labor unions have shrunk to a small percentage of the industrial and service workforce, due to corporate restructuring and job export. See *Xinhua*, January 7, 2012, "20% of Chinese Join Trade Unions." http://www.chinadaily.com.cn/china/2012-01/07/content_14400312.htm

4 IHLO (International Trade Union Confederation (ITUC)/Global Union Federation (GUC) Hong Kong Liaison Office), January 2, 2007, "ACFTU (All-China Federation of Trade Unions) Established a Union at Foxconn on the Very Last Day of 2006."
5 Foxconn's statement to the author on December 31, 2013, p. 4.

References

Andreas, Joel. 2008. "Changing Colors in China." *New Left Review* 54 (Nov/Dec): 123–42.

Appelbaum, Richard P. 2008. "Giant transnational contractors in East Asia: Emergent trends in global supply chains." *Competition & Change* 12(1): 69–87.

Appelbaum, Richard P. 2011. "Transnational Contractors in East Asia," in Gary G. Hamilton, Misha Petrovic and Benjamin Senauer (eds.), *The Market Makers: How Retailers are Reshaping the Global Economy*. Oxford: Oxford University Press, pp. 255–68.

Becker, Jeffrey. 2012. "The Knowledge to Act: Chinese Migrant Labor Protests in Comparative Perspective." *Comparative Political Studies* 45: 1379–404.

Bian, Morris L. 2009. *The Making of the State Enterprise System in Modern China: The Dynamics of Institutional Change*. Cambridge, MA: Harvard University Press.

Blecher, Marc. 2010. *China Against the Tides: Restructuring through Revolution, Radicalism, and Reform*, 3rd edn. New York: Continuum.

Braverman, Harry. 1998. *Labor and Monopoly Capital: The Degradation of Work in the Twentieth Century*. New York: New York University Press.

Burawoy, Michael. 1976. "The Functions and Reproduction of Migrant Labor: Comparative Material from Southern Africa and the United States." *American Journal of Sociology* 81(5): 1050–87.

Burawoy, Michael. 1985. *The Politics of Production: Factory Regimes under Capitalism and Socialism*. London: Verso.

Butollo, Florian and Tobias ten Brink. 2012. "Challenging the Atomization of Discontent: Patterns of Migrant-Worker Protest in China during the Series of Strikes in 2010." *Critical Asian Studies* 44(3): 419–40.

Cai, Fan. 2009. "The future of demographic dividend – Open up the origin of China's Economic Growth." *Zhongguo Renkou Kexue (The Science of China's Population)* 《中國人口科學》 1(1): 2–10 (in Chinese).

Cai, Yongshun. 2006. *State and Laid-Off Workers in Reform China: The Silence and Collective Action of the Retrenched*. London: Routledge.

Chan, Anita. 2001. *China's Workers under Assault: The Exploitation of Labor in a Globalizing Economy*. Armonk, NY: M. E. Sharpe.

Chan, Anita. 2003. "Racing to the Bottom: International Trade without a Social Clause." *Third World Quarterly* 24(6): 1011–28.

Chan, Anita. 2009. "Challenges and Possibilities for Democratic Grassroots Union Elections in China: A Case Study of Two Factory-Level Elections and Their Aftermath." *Labour Studies Journal* 34(3): 293–317.

Chan, Anita. 2011. *Walmart in China*. Ithaca, NY: Cornell University Press.

Chen, Feng. 2007. "Individual Rights and Collective Rights: Labor's Predicament in China." *Communist and Post-Communist Studies* 40(1): 59–79.

Chen, Feng. 2009. "Union Power in China: Source, Operation, and Constraints." *Modern China* 35(6): 662–89.

Chen, Feng and Xin Xu. 2012. "'Active Judiciary': Judicial Dismantling of Workers' Collective Action in China." *The China Journal* 67 (January): 87–107.

Chen, Zhiwu. 2008. *Gaige Kaifa 160 Nian (160 Years of Reform and Opening)*. Shanghai: Shanghai Renmin Chubianshi (Shanghai People's Publishing House).

Cheng, Tiejun and Mark Selden. 1994. "The Origins and Social Consequences of China's *Hukou* System." *The China Quarterly* 139 (September): 644–68.

China Labor Statistical Yearbook 2012. 2013. *Trade Union Members in Grassroots Trade Union by Region*. Beijing: China Statistics Press, pp. 405–6.

China Labor Statistical Yearbook 2013. 2014. Beijing: China Statistics Press.

Clark, Terry Nichols, and Seymour Martin Lipset. 1991. "Are social classes dying?" *International Sociology* 6(4): 397–410.

Clark, Terry Nichols, and Seymour Martin Lipset. 2001. *The Breakdown of Class Politics: A Debate on Post-Industrial Stratification*. Washington, DC: Woodrow Wilson Center Press.

Clarke, Simon, Chang-Hee Lee, and Qi Li. 2004. "Collective Consultation and Industrial Relations in China." *British Journal of Industrial Relations* 42(2): 235–54.

Cook, Sarah. 2002. "From rice bowl to safety net: Insecurity and social protection during China's transition." *Development Policy Review* 20(5): 615–35.

Culpan, Tim. 2012. "Apple Profit Margins Rise at Foxconn's Expense: Chart of the Day." *Bloomberg Business*, January 5. Available at: http://www.bloomberg.com/news/2012-01-04/apple-profit-margins-rise-at-foxconn-s-expense.html

Dang Guoying and Wenyuan Wu. 2014. "Land Planning and Management Reform: Right Adjustment and Legalistic Construction." *Faxue Yanjiu* (*Legal Studies*) 36: 57–75 (in Chinese).

Davis, Deborah S. and Feng Wang (eds.). 2009. *Creating Wealth and Poverty in Postsocialist China*. Stanford, CA: Stanford University Press.

Du, Runsheng. 2007. *Du Runsheng Zizhuan* (*Autobiography of Du Runsheng*). Beijing: Beijing Renmin Chubianshi (Beijing People's Publishing House).

Fan, C. Cindy. 2003. "Rural–Urban Migration and Gender Division of Labor in Transitional China." *International Journal of Urban and Regional Research* 27(1): 24–47.

Fan, C. Cindy. 2004. "The State, the Migrant Labor Regime, and Maiden Workers in China." *Political Geography* 23(3): 283–305.

Fang, Zhengwei. 2003. "The Private Plot: The Minimal Protection of Peasant Workers." *Sannong Zhongguo* (*Peasant Issues of China*) 1: 41–4.

Fantasia, Rick. 1988. *Cultures of Solidarity: Consciousness, Action, and Contemporary American Workers*. Berkeley, CA: University of California Press.

Foucault, Michel. 1977. *Discipline and Punish: The Birth of the Prison*. New York: Random House.

Foxconn Technology Group. 2009. "Corporate Social and Environmental Responsibility Annual Report 2008."

Foxconn Technology Group. 2010. "Corporate Social and Environmental Responsibility Annual Report 2009."

Foxconn Technology Group. 2011. "Corporate Social and Environmental Responsibility Annual Report 2010."

Foxconn Technology Group. 2012. "Corporate Social and Environmental Responsibility Annual Report 2011."

Foxconn Technology Group. 2013. "Corporate Social and Environmental Responsibility Annual Report 2012."

Foxconn Technology Group. 2014. "Foxconn Corporate Social and Environmental Responsibility Annual Report 2013," p. 14. Available at: http://ser.foxconn.com/ViewAnuReport.do?action=showAnnual

Friedman, Eli. 2014. *Insurgency Trap: Labor Politics in Postsocialist China*. Ithaca, NY: Cornell University Press.

Friedman, Eli and Ching Kwan Lee. 2010. "Remaking the World of Chinese Labour: A 30-Year Retrospective." *British Journal of Industrial Relations* 48(3): 507–33.

Fukuyama, Francis. 2006. *The End of History and the Last Man*. New York: Simon and Schuster.

Gaetano, Arianne M. and Tamara Jacka (eds.). 2004. *On the Move: Women in Rural-to-Urban Migration in Contemporary China*. New York: Columbia University Press.

Gallagher, Mary E. 2006. "Mobilizing the Law in China: 'Informed Disenchantment' and the Development of Legal Consciousness." *Law and Society Review* 49(4):783–816.

Gallagher, Mary E. and Baohua Dong. 2011. "Legislating Harmony: Labor Law Reform in Contemporary China," in Sarosh Kuruvilla, Ching Kwan Lee and Mary E. Gallagher (eds.), *From Iron Rice Bowl to Informalization: Markets, Workers, and the State in a Changing China*. Ithaca, NY: Cornell University Press, pp. 36–60.

Gao, Liang. 2009. "Globalization, Liberation of Thought and the Change of Economic Development Mode." *Kaifa Daobao (The Open Herald)*, 2009(2): 1–3 (in Chinese).

Gorz, Andre. 1997. *Farewell to the Working Class: An Essay on Post-Industrial Socialism*. London: Pluto Press.

Grush, Andrew. 2012. "iPhone 5's Killer New Feature: Scuffs, Scratches and Dents," *Mobile Magazine*, September 24. Available at: http://www.mobilemag.com/2012/09/24/iphone-5s-killer-new-feature-scuffs-scratches-and-dents/

Gu, Baochang and Yong Cai. 2011. "Fertility Prospects in China." United Nations Population Division, Expert Paper No. 2011/14.

Guang, Lei. 2005. "The Market as Social Convention: Rural Migrants and the Making of China's Home Renovation Market." *Critical Asian Studies* 37(3): 391–411.

Guthrie, Doug. 2012. *China and Globalization: The Social, Economic and Political Transformation of Chinese Society*. London: Routledge.

Han, Jun and Chuanyi Cui. 2007. "The Rising Tide of Doing Business among Returned Migrant Workers." *Zhongguo jingji shibao (China's Economic Times)*, December 27 (in Chinese).

Han, Sunsheng and George Ofori. 2001. "Construction Industry in China's Regional Economy, 1990–1998." *Construction Management and Economics* 19: 189–205.

Hardt, Michael, and Antonio Negri. 2005. *Multitude: War and Democracy in the Age of Empire*. New York: Penguin.

Harvey, David. 2007 [1982]. *The Limits to Capital*. London: Verso.

Harvey, David. 2010. *The Enigma of Capital and the Crises of Capitalism*. New York: Oxford University Press.

Harvey, David. 2014. *Seventeen Contradictions and the End of Capitalism*. New York: Oxford University Press.

Hayek, Friedrich August. 2009. *The Road to Serfdom: Text and Documents – The Definitive Edition*. Chicago, IL: University of Chicago Press.

Hershatter, Gail. 1986. *The Workers of Tianjin, 1900–1949*. Stanford, CA: Stanford University Press.

Honig, Emily. 1986. *Sisters and Strangers: Women in the Shanghai Cotton Mills, 1919–1949*. Stanford, CA: Stanford University Press.

Houtman, Dick, Peter Achterberg, and Anton Derks. 2009. *Farewell to the Leftist Working Class*. Piscataway, NJ: Transaction Publishers.

Howell, Jude A. 2008. "All-China Federation of Trade Unions beyond Reform? The Slow March of Direct Elections." *The China Quarterly* 196 (December): 845–63.

Hsing, You-tien. 1998. *Making Capitalism in China: The Taiwan Connection*. New York: Oxford University Press.

Huang, Yasheng. 2003. *Selling China: Foreign Direct Investment during the Reform Era*. Cambridge: Cambridge University Press.

Huang, Yasheng. 2008. *Capitalism with Chinese Characteristics: Entrepreneurship and the State*. Cambridge: Cambridge University Press.

Huang Zong Zhi 2000 [1992]. 《长江 三角洲小农家庭与乡村发展》 [*Development of Small Farmer Families and Villages in the Yangtze Delta*]. Beijing: Zhonghua Book Company.

Hung, Ho-fung. 2008. "Rise of China and the Global Overaccumulation Crisis." *Review of International Political Economy* 15(2): 149–79.

Hung, Ho-fung (ed.). 2009. *China and the Transformation of Global Capitalism*. Baltimore, MD: Johns Hopkins University Press.

Hurtgen, Stefanie, Boy Lüthje, Wilhelm Schumm and Martina Sproll. 2013. *From Silicon Valley to Shenzhen*. Lanham, MD: Rowman and Littlefield.

Jacka, Tamara. 2006. *Rural Women in Urban China: Gender, Migration and Social Change*. Armonk, NY: M.E. Sharpe.

Katznelson, Ira and Aristide R. Zolberg (eds.). 1986. *Working-Class Formation: Nineteenth-Century Patterns in Western Europe and the United States*. Princeton, NJ: Princeton University Press.

Kondo, Dorinne K. 1990. *Crafting Selves: Power, Gender, and Discourses of Identity in a Japanese Workplace*. Chicago, IL: The University of Chicago Press.

Kraemer, Kenneth L., Greg Linden and Jason Dedrick. 2011. "Capturing Value in Global Networks: Apple's iPad and iPhone." Available at http://econ .sciences-po.fr/sites/default/files/file/Value_iPad_iPhone.pdf

Kuruvilla, Sarosh, Ching Kwan Lee and Mary E. Gallagher (eds.). 2011. *From Iron Rice Bowl to Informalization: Markets, Workers, and the State in a Changing China*. Ithaca, NY: Cornell University Press.

Lebowitz, Michael A. 2003. *Beyond Capital: Marx's Political Economy of the Working Class*. Basingstoke: Palgrave Macmillan.

Lee, Ching Kwan. 1998. *Gender and the South China Miracle: Two Worlds of Factory Women*. Berkeley, CA: University of California Press.

Lee, Ching Kwan. 2002. "Three Patterns of Working-Class Transitions in China," in Françoise Mengin and Jean-Louis Rocca (eds.), *Politics in China: Moving Frontiers*. New York: Palgrave Macmillan, pp. 62–91.

Lee, Ching Kwan. 2007. *Against the Law: Labor Protests in China's Rustbelt and Sunbelt*. Berkeley, CA: University of California Press.

Leng, Tse-Kang. 2005. "State and Business in the Era of Globalization: The Case of Cross-Strait Linkages in the Computer Industry." *The China Journal* 53 (January): 63–79.

Leung, Pak-Nang and Pun Ngai. 2009. "The Radicalization of the New Chinese Working Class: A Case Study of Collective Action in the Gemstone Industry." *Third World Quarterly* 30(3): 551–65.

Lichtenstein, Nelson (ed.). 2006. *American Capitalism: Social Thought and Political Economy in the Twentieth Century*. Philadelphia, PA: University of Pennsylvania Press.

Lin, Yifu. 2002. "Self-Sustainable Power and the Deep Problem of Reform." *Jingji Shehui Tizhi Bijiao (The Comparison of Economic and Social Systems)*, 2: 3–10 (in Chinese).

Liu, Mingwei. 2011. " 'Where There Are Workers, There Should Be Trade Unions': Union Organizing in the Era of Growing Informal Employment," in Sarosh Kuruvilla, Ching Kwan Lee and Mary E. Gallagher (eds.), *From Iron Rice Bowl to Informalization: Markets, Workers, and the State in a Changing China*. Ithaca, NY: Cornell University Press, pp. 157–72.

Lu, Xiaobo and Elizabeth J. Perry (eds.). 1997. *Danwei: The Changing Chinese Workplace in Historical and Comparative Perspective*. New York: M.E. Sharpe.

Lu, You-Jie and Paul W. Fox. 2001. The Construction Industry in China: Its Image, Employment Prospects and Skill Requirements. Working Paper No. 180. Geneva: International Labour Organization.

Mao, Zedong. 1965 [1926]. *Selected Works of Mao Tse-Tung, Vol. 1*. Beijing: Foreign Language.

Marshall, Gordon. 1983. "Some Remarks on the Study of Working-Class Consciousness." *Politics & Society* 12(3): 263–301.

Marx, Karl. 1990 [1867]. *Capital: A Critique of Political Economy. Volume One*. Trans. Ben Fowkes. London: Penguin Classics.

Mayo, Richard E. and Gong Liu. 1995. "Reform Agenda of Chinese Construction Industry", *Journal of Construction Engineering and Management* 121(1): 80–5.

Ngok, Kinglun. 2008. "The Changes of Chinese Labor Policy and Labor Legislation in the Context of Market Transition." *International Labor and Working-Class History* 73: 45–64.

Ong, Aihwa. 1987. *Spirits of Resistance and Capitalist Discipline: Factory Women in Malaysia.* Albany, NY: State University of New York Press.

Pakulski, Jan. 1993. "The Dying of Class or Marxist Class Theory?" *International Sociology* 8(3): 279–92.

Perlin, Ross. 2011. *Intern Nation: How to Earn Nothing and Learn Little in the Brave New Economy.* London: Verso.

Perry, Elizabeth J. 1993. *Shanghai on Strike: The Politics of Chinese Labor.* Stanford, CA: Stanford University Press.

Perry, Elizabeth J. and Mark Selden (eds.). 2010. *Chinese Society: Change, Conflict and Resistance,* 3rd edn. London: Routledge.

Pringle, Tim. 2013. "Reflections on Labor in China: From a Moment to a Movement." *The South Atlantic Quarterly* 112(1): 191–202.

Pun, Ngai. 1999. "Becoming *Dagongmei*: The Politics of Identity and Difference in Reform China." *The China Journal* 42: 1–19.

Pun, Ngai. 2005. *Made in China: Women Factory Workers in a Global Workplace.* Durham, NC: Duke University Press.

Pun, Ngai. 2007. "The Dormitory Labor Regime: Sites of Control and Resistance for Women Migrant Workers in South China." *Feminist Economics* 13(3): 239–58.

Pun, Ngai and Jenny Chan. 2012. "Global Capital, the State, and Chinese Workers: The Foxconn Experience." *Modern China* 38(4): 383–410.

Pun, Ngai and Huilin Lu. 2010a. "Unfinished Proletarianization: Self, Anger and Class Action of the Second Generation of Peasant-Workers in Reform China." *Modern China* 36(5): 493–519.

Pun, Ngai and Huilin Lu. 2010b. "A Culture of Violence: The Labor Subcontracting System and Collective Actions by Construction Workers in Post-Socialist China." *The China Journal* 64: 143–58.

Pun, Ngai and Anita Koo. 2014. "A 'World-Class' (Labor) Camp/us: Foxconn and China's New Generation of Labor Migrants." *positions* 23(3): 411–35.

Pun, Ngai and Chris Smith. 2007. "Putting Transnational Labour Process in its Place: Dormitory Labour Regime in Post-Socialist China." *Work, Employment and Society* 21(1): 27–46.

Pun, Ngai, Chris Chan and Jenny Chan. 2010. "The Role of the State, Labour Policy and Migrant Workers' Struggles in Globalized China." *Global Labor Journal* 1(1): 132–51.

Pun, Ngai, et al. (eds.). 2012. *Wo Zai Fushikang (Working at Foxconn).* Beijing: Zhishi Chanquan Publishing (Knowledge Property Publishing House).

Pun, Ngai, Jenny Chan and Mark Selden. Forthcoming. *Dying for an iPhone: Foxconn and the Struggle of the New Generation of Chinese Workers.* New York: Rowan and Littlefield.

Qin, Hui. 2006. "Do Peasants Oppose Land Ownership?" *Jingji guancha bao* (*Economic Watch Newsletter*), September 4.

Qiu, Jack Linchuan. 2009. *Working-Class Network Society: Communication Technology and the Information Have-Less in China.* Cambridge, MA: MIT Press.

Robinson, Ian. 2010. "The China Road: Why China is Beating Mexico in the Competition for US Markets". *New Labor Forum* 19(3): 51–6.

Rofel, Lisa. 1999. *Other Modernities: Gendered Yearnings in China after Socialism.* Berkeley, CA: University of California Press.

Ross, Andrew. 2006. *Fast Boat to China: Corporate Flight and the Consequences of Free Trade – Lessons from Shanghai.* New York: Pantheon Books.

Sargeson, Sally. 1999. *Reworking China's Proletariat.* Basingstoke: Palgrave Macmillan.

Schram, Stuart. 1969. *The Political Thought of Mao Tse Tung.* New York: Praeger.

Scott, Robert. 2012. The China Toll: Growing US Trade Deficit with China Cost More Than 2.7 Million Jobs between 2001 and 2011, with Job Losses in Every State. Economic Policy Institute Briefing Paper #345.

Sennett, Richard and Jonathan Cobb. 1972. *The Hidden Injuries of Class.* New York: W. W. Norton.

Shaffer, Lynda. 1978. "Mao Zedong and the October 1922 Changsha Construction Workers' Strike." *Modern China* 4(4): 379–418.

Silver, Beverly J. 2003. *Forces of Labor: Workers' Movements and Globalization since 1870.* Cambridge: Cambridge University Press.

Smith, Chris. 2003. "Living at Work: Management Control and the Chinese Dormitory Labour System." *Asia Pacific Journal of Management* 20: 333–58.

Smith, Chris and Ngai Pun. 2006. "The Dormitory Labour Regime in China as a Site for Control and Resistance 1." *The International Journal of Human Resource Management* 17(8): 1456–70.

So, Alvin Y. (ed.). 2003. *China's Developmental Miracle: Origins, Transformations, and Challenges.* Armonk, NY: M. E. Sharpe.

Solinger, Dorothy J. 2009. *States' Gains, Labor's Losses: China, France, and Mexico Choose Global Liaisons, 1980–2000.* Ithaca, NY: Cornell University Press.

Taylor, Bill, Kai Chang, and Qi Li. 2003. *Industrial Relations in China.* Cheltenham: Edward Elgar.

Thireau, Isabelle and Hua Linshan. 2003. "The Moral Universe of Aggrieved Chinese Workers: Workers' Appeals to Arbitration Committees and Letters and Visits Offices," *The China Journal* 50: 83–103.

Thompson, E. P. 1966. *The Making of the English Working Class.* New York: Vintage Books.

Traub-Merz, Rudolf and Kinglun Ngok (eds.) 2012. *Industrial Democracy in China: With Additional Studies on Germany, South-Korea and Vietnam.* Beijing: China Social Sciences Press.

Vogel, Ezra F. 2011. *Deng Xiaoping and the Transformation of China.* Cambridge, MA: Belknap Press of Harvard University Press.

Walder, Andrew G. 1986. *Communist Neo-Traditionalism: Work and Authority in Chinese Industry.* Berkeley, CA: University of California Press.

Walder, Andrew G. 1991. "Workers, Managers and the State: The Reform Era and the Political Crisis of 1989." *China Quarterly* 127 (September): 467–92.

Wang, Hui. 2013. "The Crisis of Representativeness and Post-Party Politics." *Modern China* 40(2): 214–39.

Wu, Jinglian. 2006. "What Kind of Industrialization China Should Take." *Guanli Shijie (Management World)* 8: 1–7 (in Chinese).

Yan, Hairong. 2008. *New Masters, New Servants: Migration, Development, and Women Workers in China.* Durham, NC: Duke University Press.

Yao, Yang, "Neixu weishenme bu zu? – Zhongguo zengzhang moshi yu hongguan jingji xilie zhi yi" [Why is domestic demand insufficient? First in a series on macroeconomics and the Chinese development model], in *Nanfang Zhoumo [Southern Weekend]*, September 19, 2009.

Zhang, Li. 2001. *Strangers in the City: Reconfigurations of Space, Power, and Social Networks within China's Floating Population.* Stanford, CA: Stanford University Press.

Zhou, Qiren. 2008. "Ten Years of Rural Reform: Substantial Progress and Institutional Innovation." *Jiaoxue yu Yanjiu (Teaching and Research)* 5: 1–4.

Index